NATURAL RESOURCES

Water and Atmosphere

NATURAL RESOURCES

AGRICULTURE

ANIMALS

ENERGY

FORESTS

LANDS

MINERALS

PLANTS

WATER AND ATMOSPHERE

CONTENTS

Preface   vi

Acknowledgments   x

Introduction   xi

1 | Concepts of Water and Atmospheric Resources   1

2 | Influence of Water and Atmospheric Resources   28

3 | Renewable and Nonrenewable Resources   46

4 | Development of Ocean and Atmospheric Resources   73

5 | The Use and Impact of Water and Atmospheric Resources   99

6 | The Importance of Water and Atmospheric Resources   119

7 | Management of Water and Atmospheric Resources   137

8 | Conservation of Water and Atmospheric Resources   154

9 | Conclusion: The Future of Water and Atmosphere   169

Glossary   188

Further Reading   196

Index   197

PREFACE

NATURAL RESOURCES: PRICELESS GIFTS FROM THE EARTH

Mankind did not weave the web of life.
We are but one strand in it. Whatever we
do to the web, we do to ourselves . . .
All things are bound together.

—Chief Seattle

The Earth has been blessed with an abundant supply of natural resources. Natural resources are those elements that exist on the planet for the use and benefit of all living things. Scientists commonly divide them into distinct groups for the purposes of studying them. These groups include agricultural resources, plants, animals, energy sources, landscapes, forests, minerals, and water and atmospheric resources.

One thing we humans have learned is that many of the important resources we have come to depend on are not renewable. *Nonrenewable* means that once a resource is depleted it is gone forever. The fossil fuel that gasoline is produced from is an example of a nonrenewable resource. There is only a finite supply, and once it is used up, that is the end of it.

While living things such as animals are typically considered renewable resources, meaning they can potentially be replenished, animals hunted to extinction become nonrenewable resources. As we know from past evidence, the extinctions of the dinosaurs, the woolly mammoth, and the saber-toothed tiger were complete. Sometimes, extinctions like this may be caused by natural factors, such as climate change, drought, or flood, but many extinctions are caused by the activities of humans.

Overhunting caused the extinction of the passenger pigeon, which was once plentiful throughout North America. The bald eagle was hunted to the brink of extinction before it became a protected species, and African elephants are currently threatened with extinction because they are still being hunted for their ivory tusks. Overhunting is only one potential threat, though. Humans are also responsible for habitat loss. When humans change land use and convert an animal's habitat to a city, this destroys the animal's living space and food sources and promotes its endangerment.

Plants can also be endangered or become extinct. An important issue facing us today is the destruction of the Earth's tropical rain forests. Scientists believe there may be medicinal value in many plant species that have not been discovered yet. Therefore, destroying a plant species could be destroying a medical benefit for the future.

Because of human impact and influence all around the Earth, it is important to understand our natural resources, protect them, use them wisely, and plan for future generations. The environment—land, soil, water, plants, minerals, and animals—is a marvelously complex and dynamic system that often changes in ways too subtle to perceive. Today, we have enlarged our vision of the landscape with which we interact. Farmers manage larger units of land, which makes their job more complex. People travel greater distances more frequently. Even when they stay at home, they experience and affect a larger share of the world through electronic communications and economic activities—and natural resources have made these advancements possible.

The pace of change in our society has accelerated as well. New technologies are always being developed. Many people no longer spend all their time focused in one place or using things in traditional ways. People now move from one place to another and are constantly developing and using new and different resources.

A sustainable society requires a sustainable environment. Because of this, we must think of natural resources in new ways. Today, more than ever, we must dedicate our efforts to conserve the land. We still live in a beautiful, largely natural world, but that world is quickly changing. World population growth and our desire to live comfortably are exerting pressures on our soil, air, water, and other natural resources. As we destroy and fragment natural habitats, we continue to push nonhuman life into ever-smaller pockets. Today, we run the risk of those places becoming isolated islands on a domesticated landscape.

In order to be responsible caretakers of the planet, it is important to realize that we humans have a partnership with the Earth and the other life that shares the planet with us. This series presents a refreshing and informative way to view the Earth's natural resources. *Agriculture: The Food We Grow and Animals We Raise* looks at agricultural resources to see how responsible conservation, such as caring for the soil, will give us continued food to feed growing populations. *Plants: Life From the Earth* examines the multitude of plants that exist and the role they play in biodiversity. The use of plants in medicines and in other products that people use every day is also covered.

In *Animals: Creatures That Roam the Planet,* the series focuses on the diverse species of animals that live on the planet, including the important roles they have played in the advancement of civilization. This book in the series also looks at habitat destruction, exotic species, animals that are considered in danger of extinction, and how people can help to keep the environment intact.

Next, in *Energy: Powering the Past, Present, and Future*, the series explores the Earth's energy resources—such as renewable power from water, ocean energy, solar energy, wind energy, and biofuels; and non-renewable sources from oil shale, tar sands, and fossil fuels. In addition, the future of energy and high-tech inventions on the horizon are also explored.

In *Lands: Taming the Wilds,* the series addresses the land and how civilizations have been able to tame deserts, mountains, arctic regions, forests, wetlands, and floodplains. The effects that our actions can have on the landscape for years to come are also explored. In *Forests: More Than Just Trees,* the series examines the Earth's forested areas and how unique and important these areas are to medicine, construction, recreation, and commercial products. The effects of deforestation, pest outbreaks, and wildfires—and how these can impact people for generations to come—are also addressed.

In *Minerals: Gifts From the Earth*, the bounty of minerals in the Earth and the discoveries scientists have made about them are examined. Moreover, this book in the series gives an overview of the critical part minerals play in many common activities and how they affect our lives every day.

Finally, in *Water and Atmosphere: The Lifeblood of Natural Systems*, the series looks at water and atmospheric resources to find out just how these resources are the lifeblood of the natural system—from drinking water, food production, and nutrient storage to recreational values. Drought, sea-level rise, soil management, coastal development, the effects of air and water pollution, and deep-sea exploration and what it holds for the future are also explored.

The reader will learn the wisdom of recycling, reducing, and reusing our natural resources, as well as discover many simple things that can be done to protect the environment. Practical approaches such as not leaving the water running while brushing your teeth, turning the lights off when leaving a room, using reusable cloth bags to transport groceries, building a backyard wildlife refuge, planting a tree, forming a carpool, or starting a local neighborhood recycling program are all explored.

Everybody is somebody's neighbor, and shared responsibility is the key to a healthy environment. The cheapest—and most effective—conservation comes from working with nature. This series presents things that people can do for the environment now and the important role we all can play for the future. As a wise Native-American saying goes, "We do not inherit the Earth from our ancestors—we borrow it from our children."

ACKNOWLEDGMENTS

While we deal with different aspects of the atmosphere and water every day, most people are not aware of how critically important they are. We depend on them as a source of many services—some obvious, others not so obvious. Obvious uses are to provide clean drinking water, fresh air to breathe, and as a pathway of transportation. Other, subtler, values are found in their aesthetic characteristics, nutrient recycling, and carbon sequestration.

I hope to instill in you—the reader—an understanding and appreciation of these resources and their vital role in our environment. Perhaps by making you more aware of them and all that they do for each one of us every day, this book will plant the seeds for conservation of these precious resources, and encourage environmental awareness and the desire to protect and use them wisely on a long term basis—a concept called resource stewardship.

I would sincerely like to thank several of the federal government agencies that study, manage, protect, and preserve water and atmospheric resources every day. In particular, I would like to acknowledge the National Oceanic and Atmospheric Administration (NOAA), the Bureau of Land Management (BLM), the U.S. Forest Service (USFS), the National Park Service (NPS), the U.S. Department of Agriculture (USDA), the Natural Resources Conservation Service (NRCS), and the Department of Fish and Wildlife Services (FWS) for providing an abundance of learning resources about this important subject. I would also like to thank the many universities across the country, as well as private organizations, that diligently strive to protect our precious water and atmospheric resources, not only at home but also worldwide.

INTRODUCTION

Water and atmospheric resources are vital to all aspects of life. Water resources are sources of water that are useful, or potentially useful, to humans. Without water, life could not exist. Some of the many uses of water include household, agricultural, industrial, and recreational activities. Virtually all human uses of water require freshwater. Only 3%, however, of all the water on Earth is freshwater, and of this, almost 70% is frozen in glaciers and the polar ice caps. Water demand already exceeds water supply in many parts of the world. Because so little is actually available for human use, it is critical that water resources be taken care of properly in order to ensure continued availability. If water sources become polluted and unusable, the effects would negatively impact all aspects of life on Earth.

It is equally important to manage and care for our atmospheric resources. Today, many areas of the world add considerable amounts of pollution to the air. Besides the damaging effects to health, this is also having an impact on the ozone layer—the layer in the Earth's atmosphere that protects all life from harmful ultraviolet radiation. Many countries are striving today to reduce the amounts of pollutants added to the atmosphere—most notably from the burning of fossil fuels. Without proper management of atmospheric resources, many scientists predict negative changes to the Earth's climate that would upset the delicate balance of many natural systems and bring warmer temperatures, rising ocean levels, and changing precipitation patterns. This volume in the Natural Resources series is focused on the key issues at hand today in the care, management, and use of atmospheric and water resources.

Chapter 1 focuses on the basic concepts of these essential resources, such as the properties and distribution of water, properties of the atmosphere, the interaction between the water and atmosphere, the world's regional climates, and the correlation between land use and water and air quality.

Chapter 2 discusses the development and influence of atmospheric and water resources, including a comparison of prehistoric conditions to those of today; the forces that drive the motion and flow of these resources on a global basis; and their effect on navigation, settlement, and civilization.

Chapter 3 presents the types of resources—renewable and non-renewable. It looks at the critical cycles of the atmosphere and water, such as the water cycle; the various array of aquatic and atmospheric resources, such as food, transportation, minerals, power generation, ecosystems, and biodiversity; and various resources that are capable of producing sources of energy.

Chapter 4 deals with the development of atmosphere and water resources, such as hydroelectric power, wind energy, ocean energy, geothermal resources, and air-quality issues.

Chapter 5 focuses on the use of these resources and the impact on the environment. For example, it touches on the uses of freshwater, coastal impacts of land use, the threat of overfishing, implications of oil spills, the effect agriculture has on water use, severe weather and emergency preparedness, and the greenhouse effect and global climate change.

Chapter 6 discusses the importance of these resources in terms of goods and services. It explores wetlands, delicate coral reefs, tourism, recreation, medicinal resources, education, research, and employment opportunities that are tied to these resources.

Chapter 7 presents the concepts and challenges associated with the management of these resources. It looks at water quality management, coastal management, wild and scenic rivers, air pollution control, mobile sources of air pollution, thermal pollution and the heat island effect, the consequences of acid rain, and sources of indoor air pollution and what can be done to lessen their impact.

Chapter 8 outlines conservation of these precious resources, looking specifically at water conservation and how each person can help, preservation of delicate coral reef habitats, the special consideration of Antarctica, and the issues related to repairing the human-caused damage to the atmosphere's ozone layer.

Finally, Chapter 9 explores the future of the atmosphere, oceans, and other water resources. It identifies the global challenges facing us today; why the ocean is considered by many scientists to be Earth's "final frontier"; areas where future research is needed in order to preserve oceans, lakes, coasts, and air quality; and climate and the ramifications of human behavior on water and atmospheric resources.

CONCEPTS OF WATER AND ATMOSPHERIC RESOURCES

The Earth is a watery planet. In fact, **oceans** cover more than 70% of its surface. Water is present on Earth in three forms: (1) as a solid when it freezes; (2) as a liquid; and (3) as a gas when it becomes invisible water vapor in the air. The Earth's water resources make it possible for humans and all other life-forms to exist. By providing everything from drinking water to precipitation, water plays a critical role in every ecosystem.

Air is another valuable resource; like water, without it, life would not be possible. Unlike other planets in the solar system, the Earth is enveloped in an atmosphere composed of various gases that allow us to breathe.

Without these two critical resources, life could not exist on Earth. Water and the atmosphere truly are the lifeblood of living systems. This chapter focuses on the concepts of water and the atmosphere and what makes them such valuable resources. It begins by looking at the properties and distribution of water and then examines the properties of the atmosphere. It will also look at the interaction of the two resources and their roles in determining the resulting climate of the world today. Finally, it will address the effects that land use has on both water and air resources.

PROPERTIES AND DISTRIBUTION OF WATER

Water resources—rivers, lakes, and **aquifers**—supply drinking water, support industries, transport products, and provide recreational opportunities. These resources are vital to the long-term health of people and the stability of the economy. Management of these resources is a complex task that involves the cooperation of land managers, politicians, scientists, and the community.

There is no simple answer to the question "What is water?" for water means different things to different people. To most people, water is what flows from a faucet or what fills a **pond** or stream; it is the rain that makes the garden grow or that spoils an outdoor party. To a sportsman, water is a lake filled with fish or a surface on which to sail, ski, or surf. But no definition of water is complete without understanding its nature and its unusual properties.

Water makes up three-fourths of the Earth's surface and is the most common substance on Earth. Yet, as common as it is, water is also the most precious substance on Earth. Water is vital to life as we know it. In fact, water makes up two-thirds of our own bodies.

Water is the only substance on Earth that appears in all three of its natural states (solid, liquid, and gas) within the normal range of climatic conditions—sometimes at the same time. Familiar examples of water in its three natural states are rain, snow, ice, hail, and steam.

Water exhibits some unusual properties compared with similar liquids. For example, most liquids contract steadily as they freeze. Water, however, contracts to a point but begins to expand as it reaches its freezing point of 32°F (0°C). This expansion can crack sidewalks, engines, and even rocks. Because of this expansion, ice is lighter than liquid water, which is good because this causes rivers and lakes to freeze from the top down instead of from the bottom up. If freezing took place from the bottom up, some bodies of water might freeze solid, killing ⬚⬚⬚⬚ ⬚⬚⬚ would also affect th⬚ ⬚⬚⬚ ⬚⬚⬚ even in the summer mor⬚

Economy – Positive

In ice, the ⬚⬚⬚ immobile crystal struct⬚ ⬚⬚⬚ each other. When ice is w⬚ ⬚⬚⬚ mes liquid water. As a li⬚ ⬚⬚⬚ d together and can mov⬚ ⬚⬚⬚ ty to move and slide aro⬚

As water ⬚ ⬚⬚⬚ mplicated. Water boils ⬚ ⬚⬚⬚ mes water vapor. Water ⬚ ⬚⬚⬚ e below its boiling point ⬚ ⬚⬚⬚ the air as vapor. **Evapo**⬚ ⬚⬚⬚ ear after a rain. It is the water vapor in the air that gives a stick, muggy feeling on a hot, humid summer day. In a vapor, the water molecules move about rapidly with little attraction to each other.

Another unusual property of water is its heat capacity; that is, its ability to absorb heat without becoming extremely hot itself. In fact, the only other material that can hold more heat than water is ammonia. Without water in it, a pan on a burner rapidly becomes red hot and then burns black. But if water is put in the pan, the water will absorb heat from ⬚⬚⬚ ot as before, and the ter⬚

Natural Resource – Positive

amount co⬚ ⬚⬚⬚ only a small

It is wa⬚ ⬚⬚⬚ oceans a key factor in th⬚ ⬚⬚⬚ y during the day and du⬚ ⬚⬚⬚ heat slowly at night or⬚ ⬚⬚⬚ the climate from experi⬚ ⬚⬚⬚ s the Sahara in Africa or⬚ ⬚⬚⬚ moderating influence ar⬚ ⬚⬚⬚ the daytime and very co⬚

Water's unusual properties, which make it so important to life, can be attributed to its remarkable chemical characteristics. Like all matter, water is made up of atoms. Atoms attach together, or bond, to form molecules. Two hydrogen atoms bonded to an oxygen atom form a water molecule. Water has several properties that make it a unique substance.

Polarity

Even though water molecules are neutral as a whole, one end of the water molecule has a positive charge, while the other has a negative charge. The oxygen end has a slight negative charge, while the hydrogen end has a slight positive charge. Each end of a water molecule is attracted to the opposite charged end of another water molecule. Water's polarity is responsible for the "stickiness," or cohesion, between the molecules.

Capillary Action and Surface Tension

The cohesion of water causes capillary attraction, which is the ability of water to move upward in small spaces. This is what allows the water to move up the fibers of a plant, giving the plant the water it needs to survive. It also moves water upward in the soil. The cohesion of water causes surface tension, water's "invisible skin," which allows bugs like water striders to walk on water.

Solubility

Water is often referred to as the "universal solvent" because its bipolar molecule (with its positive end and negative end) enables it to dissolve a wide variety of substances. Solubility is affected by polarity. Polar substances can dissolve other polar substances; and nonpolar substances dissolve other nonpolar substances. Polar substances and nonpolar substances, however, do not mix.

Density

Another unique property of water is its density at different phases. The density of most substances increases when a liquid becomes a solid.

However, solid water is actually less dense than liquid water. This is why ice floats on water. If it didn't, frozen water in the polar regions would sink and change the ocean levels.

Seawater varies from freshwater in its composition. The table below lists the concentrations of eleven components that make up seawater.

There is an enormous amount of water locked in glaciers; stored in lakes; contained in underground reservoirs; and found in rivers, streams, oceans, and in the atmosphere. Although it may not seem like it, there are even trace amounts of water in the atmosphere over the Earth's hottest, driest regions, like Death Valley. Some of the most arid areas even contain deep underground reservoirs filled with water.

Hydrologists (scientists who study water), estimate the existence of water resources by using two different categories: (1) *known* (already

Components of Seawater

Component	Amount (grams/kilogram of water)
Chloride	19.53
Sodium	10.76
Sulfate	02.72
Magnesium	01.294
Calcium	00.413
Potassium	00.387
Bicarbonate	00.142
Bromide	00.067
Strontium	00.008
Boron	00.004
Fluoride	00.001

Source: United States Minerals Management Service

identified) reserves and (2) *unknown* (inferred) reserves. Known resources are contained in forms that can be measured and calculated, such as rivers, streams, lakes, glaciers, and oceans. Other areas are not as easy to measure. These inferred water resources are contained in locations such as deep underground reservoirs. Potential amounts are based on indirect evidence and measurements because scientists cannot get directly to the water source to measure it.

Hydrologists with the U.S. Geological Survey (USGS) have estimated that the world's total water supply is 358,964,190,061,714,300,000 gallons. If this amount of water was poured on the United States, the land surface would be submerged under 90 miles (145 kilometers) of water. Even though this may seem like a huge supply of water, it is not distributed evenly around the Earth, and some areas have so little water that droughts and other natural factors can have a serious impact on the survival of life in those regions. Humans are able to survive on a very small amount of the Earth's total water supply. In fact, usable freshwater amounts to less than 1% of the total.

The Truth About Water

- U.S. citizens use about 150 gallons (568 liters) of water per day per person for ordinary household use. Europeans use a third of this, and citizens of other nations much less.
- Renewable water resources, such as groundwater or lakes, are becoming scarce for many countries experiencing population growth.
- Water, made unsafe by human waste, industrial wastewater, pesticides, and fertilizers, represents a major global health problem as well as contributes to water scarcity.
- More than 12 million children die each year because of unsafe drinking water.

Source: U.S. Environmental Protection Agency

Oceans

The oceans, whose depth averages 12,500 feet (3,810 meters), comprise the bulk of the world's water—more than 97% of the total.

Ice Caps and Glaciers

In second place for holding the largest amount of water are the Earth's ice caps and glaciers. Roughly 7 million cubic miles (29,177,273 cubic kilometers)—equaling 2.15% of the world total—is contained in these features. Of all the frozen water, mountain glaciers (such as the Alps and Himalayan glaciers) and small ice caps are nearly insignificant compared to the amount of ice locked in the Greenland and Antarctic ice caps. According to the U.S. Environmental Protection Agency (EPA), the Greenland ice cap averages 5,000 feet (1,524 m)—which is nearly a mile in thickness—and contains a total volume of 630,000 cubic miles (2,625,955 cubic km) of water. If it were melted, it would provide enough water to maintain the current flow of the Mississippi River for more than 4,700 years.

Even more impressive is the Antarctic ice cap. Measuring up to 1,000 feet (305 m) thick in some places, this sheet of ice covers an area of about 6 million square miles (15,539,929 square km) and has a total volume of nearly 7 million cubic miles (29,177,273 cubic km)—or about 85% of all existing ice and about 64% of all water outside the oceans. If the ice cap were to melt at a constant rate, it could feed the Mississippi River for more than 50,000 years; all the rivers in the United States for about 17,000 years; the Amazon River for about 5,000 years; or all the rivers of the world for about 750 years.

Groundwater

Subsurface water, or **groundwater**, serves as a reservoir for volumes of water. There are three principal types of groundwater: vadose water (water just below the belt of soil moisture), groundwater to a depth of a half mile (2,640 feet or 805 m), and deep-lying groundwater (deeper than 2,640 feet or 805 m).

Large amounts of freshwater are locked up in glaciers and ice caps, such as the Ross Ice Shelf of Antarctica, seen above. *(Courtesy of National Oceanic and Atmospheric Administration, photo by Michael Van Woert, NOAA Corps Collection)*

Vadose water (which also includes surface moisture) is the water contained in the upper reaches of the soil. This water resource plays a very important role by supplying water to plants, which are the beginning of food chains. Most of the vegetation in the world survives on this moisture in the soil. Vadose water is also important because it serves as potential groundwater recharge, and can be extracted for use as drinking water.

Below the vadose water lies a reservoir of groundwater, which has been known to humans for thousands of years. Only recently, though, have we begun to understand what quantities of groundwater exist and how important this water is in meeting current and future water needs.

Groundwater begins as precipitation that seeps into the ground. The amount of water that seeps into the ground varies geographically, depending on factors such as the slope of the land, amount and intensity of rainfall, and type of land surface. Porous, or permeable, land that contains lots of sand or gravel will allow as much as 50% of the precipitation to seep into the ground to become groundwater. In less permeable areas, as little as 5% may seep in. The rest of the water becomes **runoff** or evaporates. More than half of the freshwater on Earth is stored as groundwater.

As water seeps through permeable ground, it continues downward until it reaches a depth where water has filled all the porous areas in the soil or rock. This is known as the saturated zone. The top of the saturated zone is called the water table. The water table can rise or fall according to the seasons of the year and the amount of precipitation that occurs. The water table is usually higher in early spring (because of melting snow) and lower in late summer. The porous area between the land surface and the water table is known as the unsaturated zone, or zone of aeration. Groundwater usually moves slowly. The rate of flow is determined by the slope of the water table and the sizes of the pores (spaces) among the rock and soil particles.

Water-bearing rock, sand, gravel, or soil that is capable of producing usable amounts of groundwater is called an aquifer. The water yield from an aquifer depends on the type of materials that it contains.

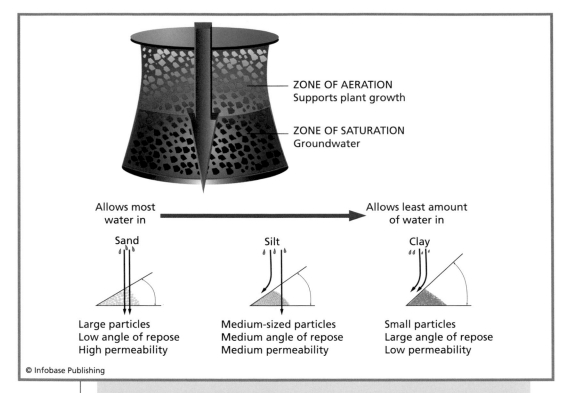

ZONE OF AERATION
Supports plant growth

ZONE OF SATURATION
Groundwater

Allows most water in →→→ Allows least amount of water in

Sand

Large particles
Low angle of repose
High permeability

Silt

Medium-sized particles
Medium angle of repose
Medium permeability

Clay

Small particles
Large angle of repose
Low permeability

© Infobase Publishing

Groundwater potential. Soils usually consist of many different-sized particles. The zone of aeration supports plant growth. It consists of open pore spaces for water, air, and plant roots to occupy. Beneath it, the zone of saturation is the area whose pore spaces are completely filled with water. Sand is the most porous soil texture and allows water to easily fill in the pore spaces. Silt, which has medium-sized particles, allows moderate percolation. Clay materials—which have the smallest particles—allow the least amount of water to percolate through the pore spaces.

Mixtures of clay, sand, and fine particles provide small amounts of water because the spaces between the particles don't allow for much water absorption and flow. Bedrock aquifers will yield enormous amounts of water if there are large openings or cracks in the rock. The capacity of soil or rock to hold water is called its *porosity*; the capacity for water to move through the aquifer is called *permeability*.

Water that seeps into an aquifer is called *recharge*. Recharge comes from several sources, such as seepage from rain and snowmelt, streams, and groundwater flow from other areas. Recharge occurs where permeable soil allows water to seep into the ground. Areas in which this occurs are called recharge areas, which can be small or large. A small recharge area may supply all the water to a large aquifer. Streams that recharge groundwater are called losing streams because they lose water to the surrounding soil or rock.

Groundwater can emerge from the ground at various discharge (exit) points. Discharge happens continuously as long as enough water is present above the discharge point. Discharge points include springs, streambeds and lakebeds, wells, ocean shorelines, and **wetlands**. Streams that receive groundwater are called gaining streams because they gain water from the surrounding soil or rock. In times of drought, most of the surface water flow can come from groundwater. Plants can also contribute to groundwater discharge, because if the water table is close enough to the surface, groundwater can be discharged by plants through transpiration.

Groundwater generally moves slowly from recharge areas to discharge points. Flow rates within most aquifers can be measured in feet per day. Flow rates are faster when cracks in rocks or very loose soil allow water to move freely.

Groundwater exists beneath most land areas of the world; even under deserts, mountain peaks, and some sub-seafloors, there is a zone where the pores of rocks and sediment are saturated with water.

Below the water table to a depth of about a half mile (800 m) in land areas of the Earth's crust, there is an estimated 1 million cubic miles (4,168,182 cubic km) of groundwater. This is 3,000 times greater than the volume of water in all rivers at any one time. An equal, if not greater, amount of groundwater is present at a greater depth down to 10,000 to 15,000 feet (3,038 to 4,572 m). Much of the deep-lying water is not economically recoverable for human use at the present time, and a good deal of it is strongly mineralized. According to the EPA, the total amount of groundwater resources on the Earth are estimated to be two-thirds of 1% of the world's water.

Lakes—Fresh and Salt

The Earth's land areas are covered with hundreds of thousands of lakes. The majority of the Earth's lake water exists in three continents—Africa, Asia, and North America.

According to the EPA, the volume of all the large freshwater lakes in the world is nearly 30,000 cubic miles (125,045 cubic km). A lake is called "large" if it contains at least 5 cubic miles (21 cubic km) of water. The largest lake is Lake Baikal in Siberia, with a volume of 6,300 cubic miles (26,260 cubic km). Lake Baikal alone contains nearly 300 cubic miles (1,250 cubic km) more water than the combined contents of the five North American Great Lakes.

Saline lakes are roughly equivalent in magnitude to freshwater lakes. Their total area is about 270,000 square miles (699,300 sq. km),

A Sampling of the World's Freshwater Lakes

Lake	Size
Baikal, Siberia	6,300 cubic miles (26,260 cubic km)
Tanganyika, Africa	5,000 cubic miles (20,841 cubic km)
Nyasa, Africa	3,200 cubic miles (13,338 cubic km)
Superior, United States and Canada	3,000 cubic miles (12,505 cubic km)
Great Bear, Canada	670 cubic miles (2,792 cubic km)
Nipigan, Canada	150 cubic miles (625 cubic km)
Vanern, Sweden	35 cubic miles (146 cubic km)
Leman, Switzerland	12 cubic miles (50 cubic km)
Tutigting, China	6 cubic miles (25 cubic km)
Dubawnt, Canada	6 cubic miles (25 cubic km)

and their total volume is about 25,000 cubic miles (104,205 cubic km). The majority of saline lakes occur in the Caspian Sea and Asia. North America's shallow Great Salt Lake is comparatively insignificant, with a volume of about 7 cubic miles (29 cubic km).

Rivers and Streams

Scientists need to differentiate between the actual amount of water present at any given time in river channels and the amounts that are discharged by rivers. According to the EPA, it has been estimated that the total amount of water physically present in stream channels throughout the world at any given moment is about 500 cubic miles (2,084 cubic km), a small fraction of the world's fresh surface water supply and only a little more than one-thousandth of the world's total supply. Some rivers are very large. For example, the Mississippi River, North America's largest river, has a drainage area of 1,243,000 square miles (3,219,370 sq. km)—about 40% of the total land area of the 48 conterminous states. It also discharges at an average rate of 620,000 cubic feet per second (17,556 cubic m/sec). This amounts to 133 cubic miles per year (554 cubic km/year).

The Amazon, the largest river in the world, is nearly 10 times the size of the Mississippi, discharging about 4 cubic miles (17 cubic km) each day or 1,300 cubic miles per year (5,419 cubic km/year)—about three times the flow of all U.S. rivers. Africa's great Congo River, with a discharge of 340 cubic miles per year (1,417 cubic km/yr), is the world's second largest river.

Estuaries

Some of the most dynamic areas on Earth are found at the interface of land and **sea**, in areas known as estuaries. Estuaries are areas of unusual activity and have production comparable to the most productive agricultural lands—more than 5 tons per acre per year. An **estuary** is a semi-enclosed coastal body of water that has a free connection with the open sea and within which seawater is measurably diluted with freshwater from land drainage. There are five important functions of estuaries:

- They provide nursery areas for 90% of the commercial seafood populations.
- They provide food for most of the seafood populations.
- They provide shelter for many small marine animals.

The Earth's Water Resources

Source	Surface area mi.^{2}/km^2	Water volume mi.^{3}/km^3	% of total water
Surface water freshwater lakes	330,000 / 854,696	30,000 / 125,045	0.009
Saline lakes	270,000 / 699,297	25,000 / 104,205	0.008
Stream channels	—	500 / 2,084	0.0001
Subsurface water, less than 1/2 mile (0.8 km) deep	50,000,000 / 129,499,406	1,000,000 / 4,168,182	.31
Subsurface water, more than 1/2 mile (0.8 km) deep	50,000,000 / 129,499,406	1,000,000 / 4,168,182	.31
Soil moisture and water in vadose zone	50,000,000 / 129,499,406	16,000 / 66,691	0.005
Glaciers/ice caps	6,900,000 / 17,870,918	7,000,000 / 29,177,273	2.15
Atmosphere	197,000,000 / 510,227,658	3,100 / 12,921	0.001
Oceans	139,500,000 / 361,303,341	317,000,000 / 1,321,313,644	97.2
Total	**494,000,000 / 2,059,081,830**	**326,074,600 / 1,359,138,227**	**100.00**

Source: National Oceanic and Atmospheric Administration

- They act as a storm buffer to prevent floods and absorb energy from storms such as **hurricanes.**
- They detoxify wastes.

The photosynthetic phytoplankton, benthic plants, and **marsh** grasses all play an important role in keeping the ocean healthy. They are all found in estuaries. Estuaries also provide needed habitat for millions of birds, both local and migratory. Many birds depend on estuaries and other wetlands for survival.

The World's Water

If a 55-gallon (208 liters) drum, filled to the brim, were to represent the world's total water supply, then . . .

- The oceans of the world would total 53 gallons, 1 quart, 1 pint, and 12 ounces (202 liters).
- The ice caps and glaciers would total 1 gallon and 12 ounces (4 liters).
- Groundwater would add up to 1 quart and 11.4 ounces (1.3 liters).
- The atmosphere would contribute 1 pint and 4.5 ounces (0.6 liters).
- Freshwater lakes would add up to half an ounce (0.01 liter).
- Saline lakes and inland seas would total one-third of an ounce (0.01 liter).
- Soil moisture and vadose water would total about one-fourth of an ounce (0.007 liter).
- The rivers of the world would measure only one one-hundredth of an ounce (0.0003 liter)—less than one one-millionth of the water on the planet.

Source: National Atmospheric and Oceanic Administration (NOAA)

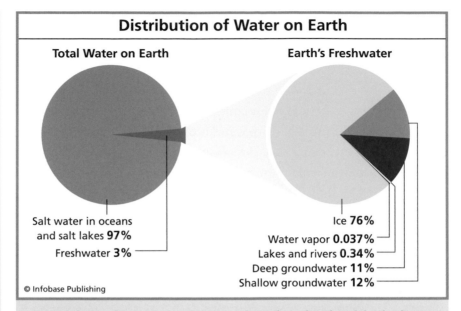

Distribution of Water on Earth

Total Water on Earth

Salt water in oceans
and salt lakes **97%**
Freshwater **3%**

Earth's Freshwater

Ice **76%**
Water vapor **0.037%**
Lakes and rivers **0.34%**
Deep groundwater **11%**
Shallow groundwater **12%**

© Infobase Publishing

Most of the Earth's water is salt water. About three-fourths of the freshwater on Earth is locked up as ice. Only the water in lakes, rivers, and shallow groundwater is available for human use, making freshwater a very valuable natural resource.

The Atmosphere

Another important component in the world's water budget is the atmosphere. Only an extremely small amount of water resides in the atmosphere at any given time. As a comparison, the volume of the lower 7 miles (11 km) of the atmosphere contains only about 3,100 cubic miles (12,921 cubic km) of water (about one-one hundredth of a percent of the world's total supply), mainly in the form of invisible vapor. According to the EPA, if all this vapor were suddenly condensed and then precipitated from the air onto the Earth's surface, it would form a layer only 1 inch (2.54 cm) thick. Although this may not seem like a lot, what makes atmospheric water so valuable is the critical role it plays in the water cycle. The water cycle is discussed in detail in Chapter 3.

Watersheds

Scientists and land managers often manage water resources based on **watersheds**. A watershed, also called a drainage basin, is the area in which all water, sediments, and dissolved materials drain from the land into a common body of water, such as a river, lake, or ocean. A watershed encompasses not only the water, but also the surrounding land from which the water drains. Watersheds can be different sizes; they can be areas as large as the Amazon River drainage basin or as small as a backyard.

Nature does not always provide the amount of water needed everywhere, when needed, or in the desired quality. Not only does nature play a part in water supply and quality, but the human demand for abundant clean water also puts a stress on the landscape and water cycle. As world populations continue to grow, increasing demand is put on the world's principal water sources. The reality is that currently 97% of all water is stored in the Earth's oceans, and most of the remaining 3% is locked up in the Antarctic and Greenland ice sheets. Humans must survive on less than 1% of the world's water that is directly available for freshwater use. Water knows no boundaries. Because the water cycle and water budget operates on a global scale, it is important that countries work together globally to make the best use of the water that is available.

PROPERTIES OF THE ATMOSPHERE

The Earth's atmosphere is a thin envelope of gases that surrounds the planet. The mixtures of gases that make up the atmosphere each have their own physical properties. Nitrogen (N_2) and oxygen (O_2) make up 99% of the volume of air. The remaining 1% is composed of "trace" gases, such as argon, carbon dioxide, and **ozone**. Even though they exist in very small amounts, the trace gases are very important to life on Earth. Water vapor, another gas, also exists in small amounts, varying in concentration depending on where it is located geographically.

The atmosphere is divided vertically into four layers—the troposphere, stratosphere, mesosphere, and thermosphere. The lowest layer

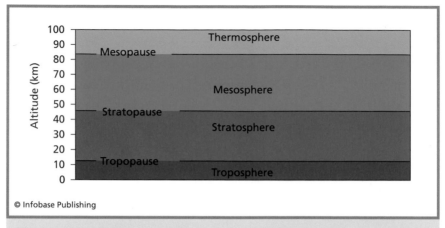

© Infobase Publishing

This graphic represents the layers of the atmosphere. The atmosphere is divided vertically into four layers. Through the troposphere, temperature decreases with altitude. This is not the case in some of the higher layers.

is the troposphere, the layer in which all of the Earth's weather occurs. The troposphere starts at the surface of the Earth and extends 7 miles (11 km) upward. In this layer, the temperature generally decreases with increasing altitude. The troposphere ends at a boundary called the tropopause.

Most of the water vapor in the atmosphere comes from oceans. The oceans and atmosphere interact extensively. Oceans not only act as an abundant moisture source for the atmosphere but also as a heat source and sink (storage). This exchange of heat and moisture has important effects on atmospheric processes near and over the oceans.

Almost all of the energy that reaches the Earth comes from the sun. Intercepted first by the atmosphere, a small part is directly absorbed, mainly by certain gases such as ozone and water vapor. Some energy is also reflected back into space by clouds and the Earth's surface. The interaction of the atmosphere and ocean and how heat is transferred worldwide is discussed later in this chapter.

An important gas in the atmosphere is ozone. Many scientists and environmentalists today are concerned about the ozone distribution in the atmosphere. Ozone is comprised of three oxygen atoms (the

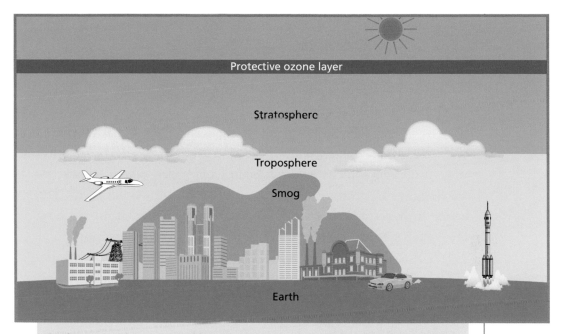

Protective ozone layer

Stratosphere

Troposphere

Smog

Earth

In the troposphere, ground-level ozone is an air pollutant that damages the health of humans and other life-forms. It is a key ingredient of urban smog. The "good" ozone, or ozone layer, exists in the stratosphere, where it protects life on Earth from the harmful effects of the sun's ultraviolet rays.

more common oxygen found in the atmosphere is made up of two oxygen atoms). When enough ozone molecules are present, it forms a pale blue gas. Ozone has the same chemical structure whether it is found in the stratosphere or the troposphere, but where it is found determines whether it is "good" ozone or "bad" ozone.

In the troposphere, the ground-level or "bad" ozone is an air pollutant that damages human health and vegetation. That ozone is a principal ingredient of urban smog. In the stratosphere is the "good" ozone that protects life on Earth from the harmful effects of the sun's ultraviolet (UV) rays.

Ozone is constantly being formed in the Earth's atmosphere by the action of the sun's ultraviolet radiation on oxygen (O_2) molecules. Ultraviolet light splits the molecules apart by breaking the bonds between the atoms. The resulting highly reactive free oxygen atom then collides with another oxygen molecule and forms an ozone molecule (O_3)—a combination of three oxygen atoms. Because ozone is unstable, ultraviolet light quickly breaks it up, and the process of creating ozone begins again.

The ozone in the stratosphere is beneficial to life on Earth because it absorbs ultraviolet light from the sun. Ultraviolet energy is short-wave radiation, which can cause skin cancer (for which sunscreens are designed to protect the skin from the sun's ultraviolet light). The ozone provides a "shield" that prevents this radiation from reaching the Earth's surface. While both oxygen and ozone together absorb 95 to 99.9% of the sun's ultraviolet radiation, only ozone effectively absorbs the two most energetic types of ultraviolet light, known as UV-C and UV-B, which cause biological damage.

Because ozone continuously breaks apart into its oxygen atoms and reforms as ozone molecules, a particular ozone molecule does not last very long. Even though this shield is constantly changing, the atmospheric chemical processes maintain a dynamic equilibrium that keeps the overall amount of ozone constant. It has not been until the last few decades that human activity has interfered with this delicate balance by adding chemicals to the atmosphere, which disrupts the natural processes.

About 90% of the ozone in the Earth's atmosphere lies in the stratosphere between 10 and 30 miles (16 and 48 km) above the Earth's surface. Ozone forms a concentrated layer in this region. Even so, it is relatively scarce; concentrations are typically 1 to 10 parts of ozone per 1 million parts of air (compared with about 210,000 parts of oxygen per 1 million parts of air).

The other 10% of the ozone in the Earth's atmosphere exists in the troposphere level at the surface of the Earth. This is the zone of "bad" ozone. Ozone in the troposphere is one of the greenhouse gases. The greenhouse effect, which will be discussed later, refers to the naturally occurring **greenhouse gases** that keep the Earth warm and allow life to flourish. Scientists are extremely concerned, however, about the warming effects of increased greenhouse gases that are caused by human activity. This ozone is also a major contributor to smog and has many serious health effects associated with it.

Often, people exposed to ozone experience recognizable symptoms, including coughing, irritation in the airways, rapid or shallow breathing, and discomfort when breathing or general discomfort in the chest. People with asthma may experience asthma attacks. When ozone levels are higher than normal, any of these symptoms may indicate that you should minimize the time spent outdoors or at least reduce your activity level to protect your health until ozone levels decline.

The EPA, along with state and local air agencies, have developed a number of tools to provide people with information on local ozone levels, their potential health effects, and suggested activities for reducing ozone exposure. The EPA has developed the Air Quality Index, or AQI, (formerly known as the Pollutant Standards Index) for reporting the levels of ozone and other common air pollutants. The index makes it easier for the public to understand the health significance of air pollution levels. Air quality is measured by a nationwide monitoring system that records concentrations of ozone and several other air pollutants at more than a thousand locations across the country.

The AQI scale has been divided into distinct categories, each corresponding to a different level of health concern. In the table on page 22, the AQI ranges are shown in the middle column, and the associated air-quality descriptors are shown in the right column. The left column shows the ozone concentrations, measured in parts per million (ppm), that correspond to each category.

In the United States, when pollutant levels are high, the states are required to report the AQI in their large metropolitan areas (populations more than 350,000). You may see the AQI for ozone reported in your newspaper, or your local television or radio weathercasters may use the AQI to provide information about the local area. The map is updated throughout the day and shows how ozone builds during hot summer days.

Ground-level ozone is created when certain pollutants, known as "ozone precursors," react in heat and sunlight to form ozone. Cars and other vehicles are the largest source of ozone precursors. Other important sources include industrial facilities; power plants; gasoline-powered mowers; and the evaporation of cleaners, paints, and other chemicals. Everyone can help reduce ozone levels by taking the following steps:

- Drive less. Instead of using a car, you may want to walk, use mass transit, or ride a bike.
- Carpool.
- Make sure your car is well tuned.
- Take care not to spill gasoline when you fill the tank of your car or lawn or recreation equipment.
- Make sure that you tightly seal the lids of chemical products—such as solvents, garden chemicals, or household cleaners—to keep evaporation to a minimum.

The best way to protect your health is to find out when ozone levels are elevated in your area and take simple precautions to minimize exposure—even when you do not feel obvious symptoms.

Ozone Concentrations and What They Mean

Ozone concentration (ppm) (8-hour average, unless noted)	Air Quality Index values	Air quality descriptor
0.0 to 0.064	0 to 50	Good
0.065 to 0.084	51 to 100	Moderate
0.085 to 0.104	101 to 150	Unhealthy for sensitive groups
0.105 to 0.124	151 to 200	Unhealthy
0.125 (8 hr.) to 0.404 (1 hr.)	201 to 300	Very unhealthy

Source: Environmental Protection Agency

THE INTERACTION OF ATMOSPHERE AND WATER

The atmosphere and water on the Earth interact on a constant basis from large scale (global) to small scale (such as those in different regions, such as the Pacific Northwest coast area). In fact, most of the water vapor in the atmosphere comes from the oceans, and most of the precipitation falling over land finds its way back to the oceans. The interaction between the two resources is critical to the life processes on Earth.

Oceans not only act as an abundant moisture source for the atmosphere but also as a heat source and sink. The exchange of heat and moisture has enormous effects on atmospheric processes near and over the oceans. **Ocean currents** play a significant role in transferring this heat poleward. Major currents, such as the northward flowing **Gulf Stream**, transport tremendous amounts of heat poleward and contribute to the development of many types of weather phenomena. They also warm the climate of nearby locations. Conversely, cold southward flowing currents, such as the California current, cool the climate of nearby locations.

Energy Heat Transfer

Most of the energy that reaches the Earth comes from the sun. Intercepted first by the atmosphere, a small part is directly absorbed, particularly by certain gases such as ozone and water vapor. Some energy is also reflected back to space by clouds and the Earth's surface. This reflectance is called *albedo*. The more clouds, the higher the albedo, and the more energy that is reflected back out into space. Energy is transferred between the Earth's surface and the atmosphere by three methods: conduction, convection, and radiation.

Conduction is the process where heat energy is transmitted through contact with neighboring molecules. Some solids, such as metals, are good conductors of heat, while others, such as wood, are poor conductors (this is why cooking pans are made out of metal). Air and water are relatively poor conductors. Because air is

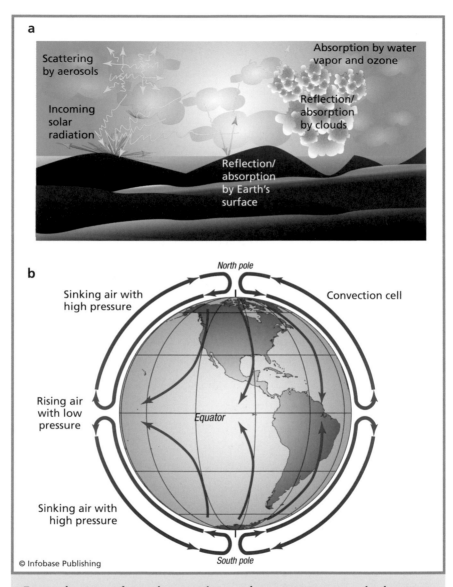

a

Scattering by aerosols

Absorption by water vapor and ozone

Incoming solar radiation

Reflection/ absorption by clouds

Reflection/ absorption by Earth's surface

b

North pole

Sinking air with high pressure

Convection cell

Rising air with low pressure

Equator

Sinking air with high pressure

South pole

© Infobase Publishing

Energy heat transfer and convection are important processes in the atmosphere. (a) Practically all of the energy that reaches the Earth comes from the Sun. Intercepted first by the atmosphere, a small part is directly absorbed. Some energy is reflected back to space by clouds and the Earth's surface. (b) Convection cells form when the unequal heating of the Earth forces air masses to rise and sink. This process plays a critical role in distributing heat over the surface of the Earth.

a poor conductor, most energy transfer by conduction occurs right at the Earth's surface. At night, the ground cools rapidly, making the cold ground conduct heat away from the adjacent air. During the day, solar radiation heats the ground, which heats the air next to it by conduction.

Convection transmits heat by transporting groups of molecules from place to place within a substance. Convection occurs in fluids such as water and air, which move freely. In the atmosphere, convection includes both large- and small-scale rising and sinking of air masses. These vertical motions are efficient at transferring heat and moisture throughout the atmosphere. Convection also contributes to cloud and storm development.

The illustration on page 24 is a simplified model of convection cells that would occur on a smooth Earth with (1) no interaction between the land and ocean and (2) a slow rotation, where the **equator** is warmed by the sun more than the poles. The warm, buoyant air at the equator rises and spreads northward and southward, and the cool dense air at the poles sinks and spreads toward the equator. As a result, convection cells are formed, like a conveyor belt.

The slow rotation of the Earth toward the east causes the air to be deflected toward the right in the Northern Hemisphere and toward the left in the Southern Hemisphere. This deflection of the wind by the Earth's rotation is called the **Coriolis effect**.

Radiation is the direct transfer of heat energy. Energy travels from the sun to the Earth by means of electromagnetic waves. The shorter the wavelength, the higher the energy associated with it.

Most of the sun's radiant energy is concentrated in the visible and near-visible portions of the spectrum. Shorter-than-visible wavelengths account for a small percentage of the total but are extremely important because they have much higher energy. These are known as ultraviolet wavelengths. The structure of the atmosphere; the interaction of gases with solar energy; and the interactions between the atmosphere, land, and oceans all work together to make life on Earth possible.

THE WORLD'S CLIMATES

The Earth's climate is usually defined as the average weather over a long period of time. A place or region's climate is determined by both natural and anthropogenic (human-made) factors. The natural elements include the atmosphere, geosphere (landforms), hydrosphere (water), and biosphere (life-forms), while the human factors can include the uses of land and resources. Changes in any of these factors can cause local, regional, or even global changes in the climate. For example, the things that determine an area's climate are factors such as major wind patterns that distribute hot and cold air around the Earth and moisture in the atmosphere, mountains, vegetated areas, tropical zones, deserts, and other features such as mountain ranges (geosphere), oceans, lakes, ice, humidity (hydrosphere), and presence of vegetation and other life-forms (biosphere).

While all these factors play a key role in the climate of a particular location, the atmosphere and water play an enormous role. Changes in these resources—whether human-caused or natural—can have major consequences on the resulting climate of an area. This is why scientists and other environmentalists are concerned about pollution, the greenhouse effect, and resulting climate change.

LAND USE AND WATER AND AIR QUALITY

Land use can have a tremendous effect on water and air quality. Farmlands can be the source of sediment, fertilizer, pesticides, and animal waste pollution that can contaminate water supplies. When forests are cut down, they can be major sources of sediment pollution in water sources. Cities pose numerous water quality problems due to the demand for clean water, industrial and commercial pollutants, human and pet wastes, and urban runoff from lawns and paved areas. Therefore, when it is decided to use land for a specific purpose, the water and air quality of an entire watershed must be taken into account and managed properly. This means considering the amount of water available as well as how it must be processed before and after use. For example, agricultural areas can require huge amounts of water for crops to grow. If there is not enough rainfall to support their growth, crops must be irrigated, which means transporting water from lakes, streams, or wells. Irrigation may require so much water that aquatic life in lakes and streams may be adversely impacted, or the water table may be lowered, causing wells and wetlands to dry up.

Certain land use practices can minimize negative impacts to the environment. For example, planting trees and other vegetation to protect soil and reduce erosion; fencing livestock to prevent access to streams; properly treating animal wastes; minimizing use of fertilizers and pesticides; properly treating all waste products from industries; using less harmful chemicals and other products in homes, businesses, and industries; and reducing, reusing, and recycling commercial products can all help reduce water pollution. Air pollution can also be reduced by monitoring and controlling industrial processes, using less fossil fuels for transportation and power generation, and relying more on renewable forms of energy.

INFLUENCE OF WATER AND ATMOSPHERIC RESOURCES

The Earth's atmosphere and water resources have had an influence on life throughout history. As these resources have changed, conditions on Earth have also changed. The interaction between these two resources and their influence on other resources is not constant—it is always changing, causing life-forms to continually adapt to current conditions or perish. This chapter examines the atmospheric and water resources on Earth during prehistoric times and outlines the physical evidence scientists can use to determine prehistoric conditions. It looks at conditions today, as well as the forces that drive this complex system. It then addresses the role these two resources have had on navigation, settlement, and civilization over time.

PREHISTORIC CONDITIONS

Atmospheric and water conditions were much different billions of years ago. The atmosphere on Earth had a drastically different chemical composition, and the oceans, as we know them today, did not exist.

Although the Earth had an atmosphere billions of years ago, it was composed primarily of methane, nitrogen, and hydrogen. Oxygen—necessary to sustain life—did not exist at that point. It was not until the development of algae, plants, and trees that the air became something that animals (including humans) could breathe.

Plants produce energy to live and grow, and as they do, they manufacture oxygen (O_2) and use up carbon dioxide (CO_2). Humans and other animals are the opposite—they use up oxygen and manufacture carbon dioxide. Because of this, the presence of trees and other vegetation is critical to supplying oxygen for the survival of other life-forms.

According to experts at the U.S. Geological Survey (USGS), scientists believe that as the Earth formed about 4 billion years ago, its primitive atmosphere contained many chemicals that would have poisoned humans. Among these chemicals, however, were the basic gases needed to form water. As the Earth cooled from a mass of molten rock, water formed in the atmosphere; then it began to rain. Scientists now believe that it rained for many, many years as the Earth continued to cool and the atmosphere we know today began to take shape. The rain came in such a large quantity that the low places on the Earth's surface were covered by water to a great depth and the oceans were formed.

Ever since the rain began to fall, and the oceans were formed, water has been trying to mold the Earth into a smooth surface through the process of erosion. Other forces within the Earth keep raising up new hills and mountains; otherwise, the Earth eventually would be covered by one vast shallow ocean.

The continents and distribution of oceans changed over time. As land-masses drifted due to plate tectonics, new oceans opened up and old ones disappeared. Earth's oceans looked much different millions of years ago. According to the theory of plate tectonics—or continental drift—the world was made up of a single continent, called Pangaea, through most of geologic time. Pangaea eventually separated and drifted apart forming the seven different continents that we have today. The positions of the continents are not rigidly fixed, but move at a slow rate—roughly 3 feet (1 meter) per century, or about as fast as a human fingernail grows.

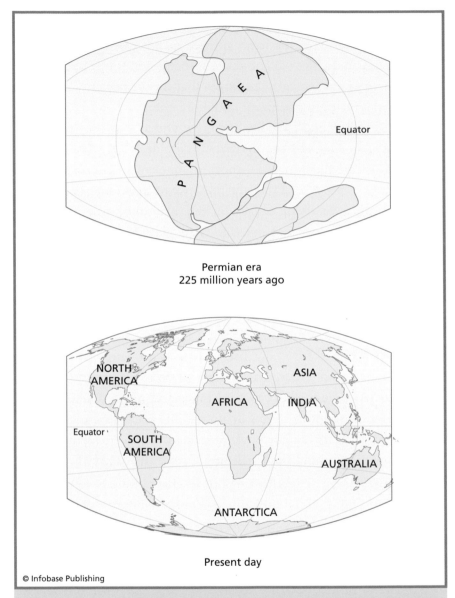

Permian era
225 million years ago

NORTH
AMERICA

ASIA

AFRICA

INDIA

Equator

SOUTH
AMERICA

AUSTRALIA

ANTARCTICA

Present day

© Infobase Publishing

The shape and distribution of the oceans have changed significantly over geologic time. The continents were once a single landmass called Pangaea. Over time, the continent broke apart and drifted, and the original single ocean, called Panthalassa, began to change. Over time, the oceans as we know them were formed. The continents, still drifting today, are controlled by the process of plate tectonics.

It was not until the 1960s, that geologists gained the technology to understand the processes at work that could move the Earth's plates. The concepts of seafloor spreading and plate tectonics emerged as powerful new hypotheses to explain the features and movements of the Earth's surface and the distribution of the oceans.

Once scientists figured out how the plates were moving, they were able to determine how the areas of ocean and landmasses have gradually changed over millions of years. As the oceans changed, so too did life within the oceans. Simple organisms first appeared 3.3 billion years ago and were followed by more and more complex life-forms. Some life-forms became extinct over time, while others—like sharks—adapted to changing conditions and still survive in the oceans today, more or less unchanged from their initial appearance.

EVIDENCE OF PAST CONDITIONS

Scientists are able to understand what conditions were like on Earth millions of years ago by studying specific indicators related to the water and atmosphere. For example, varve analysis gives clues as to the role of water in shaping past landforms; indirect biological evidence can reveal past climate; other indicators can portray evidence of past ice ages; evidence of oceans and seas once existing in areas that are dry and mountainous today can be interpreted; areas where rivers once carved their impression on the landscape can be studied; and areas where groundwater played a significant role beneath the surface of the Earth tell their own story.

A varve is an annual layer of sediment or sedimentary rock; varve analysis is the process of counting varves—or annually laminated sediments—to determine the rates of change in climate and various ecosystems. Varves are usually associated with glacial lakes. Layers of sediment form on the floor of the body of water. They form two distinct annual layers: (1) a thick, light-colored layer of silt and fine sand, which forms in the spring and summer; and (2) a thin, dark-colored layer of clay forming in the fall and winter.

The presence of varves gives scientists a glimpse into the climatic conditions of an area. When areas were cold enough to support glaciers, varves would form in adjacent lakes. Understanding the climate,

Scientists can study tree rings in order to determine what past water and atmospheric conditions were like on Earth. Thick annual rings indicate a greater amount of moisture and moderate temperatures; while thin annual rings represent years with lower available water resources and more extreme atmospheric conditions. *(Photo courtesy of Nature's Images)*

in turn, gives scientists reliable information about the water and atmospheric conditions at that time.

Significant advances have been made in the past few years to improve accuracy when interpreting varves. Using audio and visually equipped computers and digital video cameras, scientists can see and analyze the differences in hues. Many specialists view varves as one of the most important studies of past climate change. They can also be closely correlated to tree-ring analysis.

By studying biological evidence—such as tree-ring patterns—scientists also gain a clearer understanding of the roles of water and atmosphere in ancient times. Typically, years of ample rainfall and mild temperatures encourage tree growth. The annual ring portraying

Glaciers flowing down canyons carve out huge amounts of rock and debris and change the canyon's shape from V-shaped (shaped by rivers) to U-shaped as the ice scours the canyon walls. Climatologists use this type of geomorphic evidence to study past climate and understand what conditions were like on Earth long ago. *(Photo courtesy of Nature's Images)*

that year's growth will be fairly thick. Conversely, in years with little rainfall or harsh temperatures, the tree will be stressed and will show a narrower ring for that year. By analyzing the widths of the rings and counting the age of the tree (each ring represents one year), it is possible to reconstruct past conditions on Earth.

Studying climate change—such as the little ice age that occurred from A.D. 1350 to 1900—also gives scientists a broad and realistic view of past atmospheric and water conditions. Climate change can be measured by calculating shifts in the Earth's rotational axis and the changes in the shape of the Earth's elliptical orbit around the sun. Scientists believe these orbital shifts caused ice ages to begin and end over time, thereby affecting atmospheric and water resources.

The shoreline of ancient Lake Bonneville can be seen as a horizontal line halfway up the mountain in this photo. This shoreline created a "bench" that many homeowners build their houses on today. The geologic material below the shoreline is composed of sands and gravels that were deposited in the lake from rivers flowing from the mountains adjacent to the lake. Evidence such as this tells scientists that significant water resources existed in the past that are no longer there. (Courtesy of Nature's Images)

Evidence of past glaciation—such as distinctive U-shaped valleys and erratic deposits of large boulders—tell their own story about the conditions of these resources. Also important for the information they portray are ancient lake levels carved into mountains. Past evidence of an ancient lake is sometimes visible as a horizontal shoreline where no water exists today. This indicates that the past was much wetter than the conditions that exist today. The same holds true for coral deposits or fossils of sea life that are found isolated on mountains today. Evidence such as this can be gathered to support the theories that describe past oceans and wetter climates. It can also serve as an indicator of plate tectonics and the direction the plates have moved—for example, coral deposits found today on arctic mountains or in massive inland deserts (such as the Sahara). Old riverbeds can also be used to reconstruct past conditions by providing evidence of areas that once had plentiful water.

Caves are another indicator of past water conditions. They are formed by the subsurface action of water, like a type of huge subterranean plumbing system. Many massive subterranean cave systems—such as Carlsbad Caverns in New Mexico—exist throughout the world where water does not currently flow today, but did in the past.

Caves initially form from the dissolving of carbonate rocks. This occurs in the area just below the water table in the zone of saturation where the continuous mass movement of water occurs.

The second stage in cave development occurs after a lowering of the water table. During this stage, the solution cavities (the hollow openings left after the removal of the calcium carbonate in limestone by carbonic acid) are abandoned in the unsaturated zone where air can enter. This leads to the deposition of calcite, which forms a variety of dripstone features.

The chemical process causing deposition of calcite is the reverse of the process of solution. Water in the unsaturated zone, which dissolved some calcite as it trickled down through the limestone above the cave, is still enriched with carbon dioxide when it reaches the ventilated cave. The carbon dioxide gas then escapes from the water, reducing the **acidity** of the water, and calcite is deposited as dripstone.

CONDITIONS TODAY

From the seashore to the deepest depths, the oceans provide a home to some of the most diverse life on Earth, but life is not found uniformly throughout. Plants grow in the zones that receive sunlight for photosynthesis. Some animals live either on the seabed or in midwater, where they can swim or float. Most animals live in the sunlit zone, where food

Caves indicate the presence of subterranean water at some time during the past. This intricate cave formation is in Carlsbad Caverns National Park, New Mexico. *(Photo courtesy of the National Park Service)*

is plentiful, but not all free-swimming animals stay in one zone. For instance, whales can dive to depths of more than 1,600 feet (488 m) to feed on squid and then return to the surface to breathe (because they are mammals). Some animals migrate great distances during the course of a year. For example, humpback whales spend the summer feeding off the coast of Alaska and then migrate off the coast of Hawaii during the winter months. They repeat this cycle every year.

Many species dwell on the bottom of the ocean. A single area can provide a home for many life-forms, including coral, sponges, mollusks, and several species of fish.

The seabed is not flat, but has features similar to those found on dry land, such as mountains, plateaus, plains, slopes, **ridges**, rises, volcanoes, and **trenches**. Each of these areas has its own specific characteristics and life-forms, as well.

Continents end with a **continental shelf** of varying widths. The major fisheries of the world are found in these areas. The shelves end with shelf breaks and transition into continental slopes, then continental rises. It is the shelves, slopes, and rises that comprise the area known as the continental margin. Beyond this is the **abyssal plain**.

The shallow waters above the continental shelf are called the sublittoral zone. This zone is rich with life because of the available sunlight. Beyond the shelf break in the open sea, it is bright to a depth of 660 feet (200 m). This is the pelagic zone, a layer rich in **plankton** (which animals such as whales feed on) and other marine life. Below this is the bathyal zone, which goes to the bottom of the continental slope, to a depth of 6,600 feet (2,000 m). Only blue light reaches this far, but many forms of animal life exist here. Below the bathyal zone is the abyssal zone, the deepest and darkest zone of the ocean. The temperature here is only 39°F (4°C), and the pressure is tremendous, but many animals have adapted to live in this zone.

Underwater mountains are called **seamounts**. They are found in all oceans. **Guyots** are the flattened remains of islands. Seamounts and guyots cause cold, nutrient-rich currents to rise to the surface of the ocean, where light penetrates. This is an area where plankton thrives.

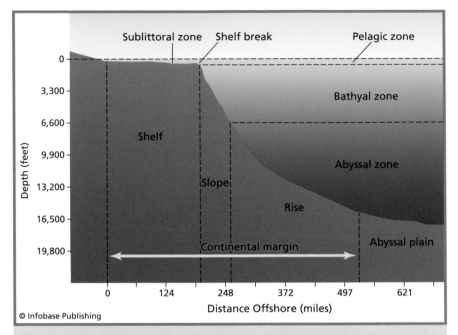

The ocean is divided into broad zones according to depth. The various zones have their own distinct topography and characteristics, from the surface down to the abyssal plain.

The shallow waters over the continental shelf are the richest areas of life in the ocean. Referred to as the light zone, light is able to penetrate as deep as 3,300 feet (1,000 m). Small plants, like phytoplankton, use the sunlight, water, and carbon dioxide to make food. The phytoplankton form the basic food source for other surface dwellers, who, in turn, are eaten by other creatures in the ocean food chain.

Coral polyps are tiny animals that live together in colonies. They secrete calcium carbonate, which forms a hard, limestone skeleton around their soft bodies. New polyps grow on the skeletons of dead polyps, forming **coral reefs**. Coral reefs support a tremendous variety of life, such as crabs, sea turtles, sea snakes, clams, and a multitude of colorful fish. Reefs are very fragile ecosystems and can be easily harmed by water pollution.

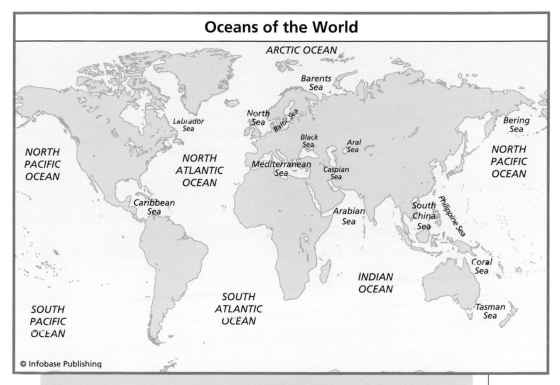

Oceans of the World

ARCTIC OCEAN

Barents Sea

North Sea

Baltic Sea

Labrador Sea

Black Sea

Aral Sea

Bering Sea

NORTH PACIFIC OCEAN

NORTH ATLANTIC OCEAN

Mediterranean Sea

Caspian Sea

NORTH PACIFIC OCEAN

Caribbean Sea

Arabian Sea

South China Sea

Philippine Sea

Coral Sea

INDIAN OCEAN

SOUTH ATLANTIC OCEAN

SOUTH PACIFIC OCEAN

Tasman Sea

© Infobase Publishing

The major oceans of the world. Oceans are the largest bodies of water; seas are typically smaller.

At the deepest areas of the ocean, where there is no light, a collection of odd creatures exist. Some—like the viperfish—have huge mouths that can eat creatures bigger than themselves. Others have body parts that glow in the dark to attract prey, a capability called bioluminescence. Many creatures that live in these dark waters are able to produce light by various biological methods.

The Pacific Ocean is bounded on the east by the Americas and on the west by Asia and Australia. At the equator, its widest point, it stretches more than halfway around the world. It covers more than a third of the Earth's surface—about 64 million square miles (166 million sq. km). The Pacific Ocean is larger than all the Earth's other oceans combined.

The Atlantic is the second largest ocean, with an area of 33 million square miles (82 million sq. km). At its widest point, it spans a distance of 5,500 miles (8,800 km) between North America and Europe. The Indian Ocean is the third largest ocean, covering an area 28 million square miles (73.3 billion sq. km) in size. These three oceans have an average depth of 12,000 feet (3,658 m).

The smallest and shallowest of the world's oceans is the Arctic Ocean, covering about 5 million square miles (13 million sq. km). Bordered mostly by land, its average depth is about 4,000 feet (1,219 m).

FORCES THAT DRIVE THE CURRENTS

The atmosphere and oceans work closely together. The temperature in seawater varies, depending on its location—from 30°F (–2°C) to 88°F (30°C). It is colder at the surface in polar regions than in the tropics. Generally, seawater gets colder with depth. The salinity (salt content) of ocean water is also variable. The average salinity is 3.5%. Saline water is denser than freshwater. The density of seawater is one of the reasons why water circulates continuously in currents. Cold, dense water sinks; warm, less-dense water flows on the surface.

As we saw in the last chapter, the sun also warms the Earth unevenly. About three times more heat arrives at the equator than at the North and the South Poles. Atmospheric winds and ocean currents absorb heat in equatorial regions and lose it as they move toward cooler regions. Steady (prevailing) winds, which blow most of the time, for most of the year, cause surface currents in the ocean. The rotation of the Earth causes these currents to veer from their paths. To the north of the equator, they curve to the right; to the south, they curve to the left. There are also other currents that flow deep down in the oceans, often in the opposite direction to currents on the surface.

Cold currents bringing water from the poles to the equator match warm currents flowing away from the equator. Cold water is heavier than warm water. Continual cooling at the poles causes the water there to sink. The deep water moves slowly. In fact, it may take hundreds of years on its journey, but some of the water comes to the surface in

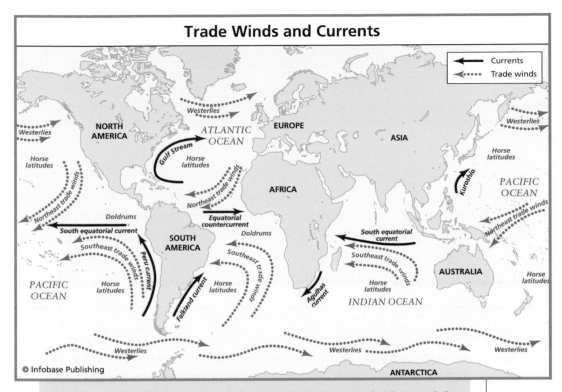

Trade Winds and Currents

The interaction of the atmosphere and water, along with the forces of the Earth's rotation, create distinct currents in the oceans and atmosphere. These currents control the Earth's heat distribution and budget. They also provide for navigation, trade, and settlement of civilization.

places. This rising is due to offshore winds that push the top layer of water away from the land. The deep, cold water wells up to replace it and continues to drift, as surface currents, toward the equator. The warm and cold currents form vast spirals of water on both sides of the equator in the Pacific, Atlantic, and Indian Oceans.

Due to the forces of this movement, wind and weather patterns are tied to the geography of the oceans. These two resources are what create the heat budget of the Earth, which allows all the different ecosystems to survive.

Just as the ocean currents move in specific patterns, distributing heat around the globe, so do global wind patterns. Hot air rises at the equator and flows toward the poles. As it travels, it cools and sinks back to the water's surface at around 30° degrees north **latitude** when heading north, and at 30° south latitude, when heading south. The air then heads toward the equator again. The circulation pattern in these two bands is known as the "trade winds," a name derived from the fact that this wind pattern made it easy for sailing ships to travel across the oceans for trade in the past.

A similar wind pattern exists between the 30° and 60° north and south latitudes. The winds here are called the "westerlies" because they blow from west to east. In the southern hemisphere, there is very little land to get in the way of the wind. For this reason, the southern westerlies can blow consistently at more than 40 miles (64 km) an hour, which is why their nickname is the "roaring forties."

The area along the equator is called the "doldrums." These winds blow slightly or not at all. Sailing ships that sailed into the doldrums would often be stalled for weeks because there was no wind to move them. A similar area of light wind lies between the trade winds and westerlies, in both the Northern and Southern hemispheres. These areas are called the "horse latitudes." Explorers sailing from Spain to the Americas crossed the northern horse latitude. Spanish explorers often took their horses with them, which is where the name came from.

The winds shown on the trade winds and currents map on page 41 are called "prevailing winds." These are winds that blow consistently from one direction and can be counted on by sailors trying to navigate a course across the oceans.

Because the wind and ocean currents are tightly linked, air and water temperature affect the weather. Water heats up and cools down more slowly than land. This means that in winter, the water is warmer than the land, and in summer, it is cooler. As a result, coastal areas generally have cooler summers and warmer winters than inland regions.

Air temperature also affects precipitation. The warmer the air, the more moisture it can hold. The warmest, wettest air is found along the

Ports provide for the bulk of the world's trade and commerce. The harbor seen here is in Seattle, Washington. *(Courtesy of National Atmospheric and Oceanic Administration)*

equator over the oceans. As this air moves over nearby land, the moisture is lost as rain, making coastal regions near the equator among the wettest places on Earth. Coastal areas, in general, tend to be wetter than inland areas because air coming off the ocean loses moisture as it travels inland. The interaction of air and water temperatures has also played a significant role in settlement patterns and the development of civilization.

NAVIGATION, SETTLEMENT, AND CIVILIZATION

For thousands of years, people have lived by the sea so that they can fish and earn a living. Today, 60% of the world's population lives on, or near, the coast. The beginnings of civilization began around major bodies of water and large rivers. One of the most well-known examples is the beginning of Egyptian civilization and its development along the Nile River. The Nile was instrumental in allowing Egyptian civilization to grow. The water supported their agriculture and provided drinking water and water for animals, as well as routes for trade. In fact, without the Nile, permanent settlements would have been almost impossible in that region.

Today, ports and harbors provide many critical services. They are critical areas of commerce, providing for most of the world's trade. They are also important for transportation routes, not only as ocean harbors, but in riverways as well. Ports and harbors serve as strategic locations for military activity. The U.S. Navy has several critical military operations in strategic locations, such as those in San Diego, California, and Pearl Harbor, Oahu, Hawaii. Settlements along coasts and other waterways are critical not only for offensive military action but also as strategic defense positions for homeland security and protection.

Large ports at the edges of the oceans handle most of the world's trade. The world's busiest port is Rotterdam, in the Netherlands, near the mouth of the river Rhine. Other ports are in natural **bays** along coasts, where ships can be sheltered from the open sea. San Francisco Bay, which contains several major ports, is the world's largest natural bay.

Major Ports of the World

This map depicts the world's ports that handle most of the ocean-going trade around the world.

Recreation and aesthetic value are other assets of port locations. Oceans and lakes provide recreational opportunities, such as boating, fishing, water skiing, sailing, **scuba** diving, surfing, swimming, and beach-combing. They also provide popular key destinations for the cruise line industry. The natural beauty of oceans and beach settings provides an aesthetic value that is hard to rival—a unique natural resource.

RENEWABLE AND NONRENEWABLE RESOURCES

There are numerous natural resources associated with the water and atmosphere that fall into two general classes: renewable and nonrenewable. A renewable resource is a resource that can be replenished. It is a resource that can be replaced through natural ecological cycles, Earth system cycles, and good management practices. The opposite of this is a nonrenewable resource—a resource that cannot be replenished. For practical applications, scientists consider a renewable resource one that can be replenished within one generation (approximately 20 to 30 years).

This chapter examines the critical Earth cycles that have a direct, significant effect on the atmosphere and water. It first looks at the role of the water, carbon, and nitrogen cycles, and then examines the multitude of natural resources that are available every day, as well as which ones are renewable and which are not.

CRITICAL CYCLES OF THE EARTH'S ATMOSPHERE AND WATER

The Earth's air, water, energy, chemical compounds, and life-forms all function together in cycles. Certain substances move endlessly through the Earth's atmosphere, hydrosphere (areas of water), lithosphere (landscape), and biosphere (living organisms). Three of the most important cycles are the water, carbon, and nitrogen cycles.

The Water Cycle

The water cycle describes the movement of all the water on Earth. It has no starting point, and involves the existence and movement of water on, in, and above the Earth. The Earth's water is always moving and changing states—from liquid to vapor to ice and back again. It has been working for billions of years, and all life on Earth depends on its continued existence. The sun ultimately drives the cycle. Over time, all water keeps moving through different components of the water cycle, including the following:

- Water storage in oceans
- Evaporation
- Evapotranspiration
- Water in the atmosphere
- Condensation
- Precipitation
- Water storage in ice and snow
- Snowmelt runoff to streams
- Surface runoff
- Stream flow
- Freshwater storage
- Infiltration
- Groundwater storage
- Groundwater discharge
- Springs

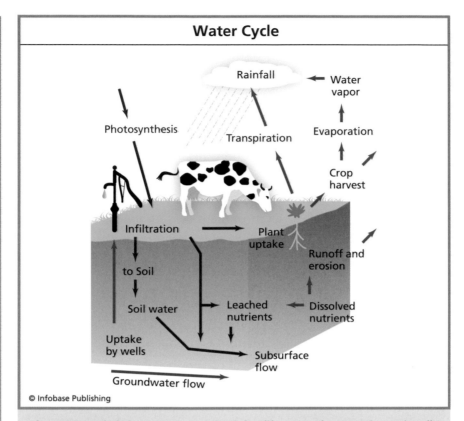

Water Cycle

Rainfall

Water vapor

Photosynthesis

Transpiration

Evaporation

Crop harvest

Infiltration

Plant uptake

to Soil

Runoff and erosion

Soil water

Leached nutrients

Dissolved nutrients

Uptake by wells

Subsurface flow

Groundwater flow

© Infobase Publishing

The water cycle is important to maintaining life on Earth. Water is continually cycling through the atmosphere, hydrosphere, lithosphere, and biosphere.

Evaporation is the process by which water changes from a liquid to a gas or vapor. Evaporation is the primary pathway that water moves from the liquid state back into the water cycle as atmospheric water vapor. Studies have shown that the oceans, seas, lakes, and rivers provide nearly 90% of the moisture in our atmosphere via evaporation, with the remaining 10% being contributed by plant transpiration.

The process of evaporation drives the water cycle. Evaporation from the oceans is the primary mechanism supporting the surface-to-atmosphere portion of the water cycle. The large surface area of the oceans provides the opportunity for such large-scale evaporation to occur. On a global scale, the amount of water evaporating is about the same as the amount of water delivered to the Earth as precipitation. This, however, varies geographically. Evaporation is more prevalent over the oceans than precipitation, while over the land, precipitation exceeds evaporation. Ocean evaporation is so great that without precipitation runoff and discharge from aquifers, oceans would become nearly empty.

Evapotranspiration represents the water lost to the atmosphere from the ground surface, evaporation from the capillary fringe of the groundwater table, and the transpiration of groundwater by plants whose roots tap the capillary fringe of the groundwater table. It is estimated that about 10% of the moisture found in the atmosphere is released by plants through transpiration. During a growing season, a leaf will transpire many times more water than its own weight. For example, a large oak tree can transpire 40,000 gallons (151,000 liters) per year.

Water is also stored in the atmosphere as vapor in the forms of clouds and humidity. Although the atmosphere may not be able to store excessive amounts of water, it is the efficient medium used to move water around the globe. There is always water in the atmosphere. Clouds are the most visible evidence of atmospheric water, but even clear air contains water that exists in particles that are too small to be seen. The atmosphere only stores about 0.001% of the Earth's total water volume.

Condensation is the opposite of evaporation. It is the process in which water vapor in the air is changed into liquid water. Condensation is crucial to the water cycle because it is responsible for the formation of clouds. These clouds may produce precipitation, which is the primary route for water to return to the Earth's surface within the water cycle. Precipitation is the water released from clouds in the form of rain, sleet, snow, or hail. It is the primary connection in the water cycle that delivers water from the atmosphere to the Earth. Most precipitation falls as rain.

Water is also stored in ice and snow—in glaciers, ice fields, and snowfields. More water is in storage on the Earth at any one time than

River levels are highest in the spring when winter snowmelt from mountains flows down rivers, where it is often stored in reservoirs to be used for water supplies during the rest of the year. The river channel completely fills with water during the spring (April and May), but by August, after the runoff has already passed through, the channel is nearly empty. *(Photo courtesy of Nature's Images)*

is actually moving through the cycle. Water in storage is water that is locked up in its present state for a relatively long period of time, such as in ice caps and glaciers. (The vast majority—almost 90%—of the Earth's ice mass is in Antarctica.)

Snowmelt runoff to streams is another important part of the water cycle. Most snowmelt runoff to streams occurs in the spring as the snow that has been stored up in the mountains begins to melt. Runoff from snowmelt varies by season, as well as by year. For example, if a major drought occurs, runoff levels are lower than those of a wetter winter. The lack of water stored as snowpack in the winter can affect the availability of water in streams for the rest of the year. This can have an effect on the amount of water in reservoirs located downstream, which

Freshwater Resources

Water source	Water volume, in cubic miles	Water volume, in cubic kilometers	Percent of freshwater
Ice caps, glaciers and permanent snow	5,773,000	24,064,000	68.5
Groundwater	2,526,000	10,530,000	30
Ground ice and permafrost	71,970	300,000	0.8
Lakes	42,320	176,400	0.5
Soil moisture	3,959	16,500	0.05
Atmosphere	3,095	12,900	0.04
Swamp water	2,752	11,470	0.03
Rivers	509	2,120	0.006
Biological water (plants/animals)	269	1,120	0.003
Total	**8,423,874**	**35,114,510**	**100**

in turn can affect the water that is available for irrigation and the water supply for cities and towns. In addition to melting snowpack, precipitation from storms can also contribute to increased stream flow.

Surface runoff is another component of the water cycle. When rain hits saturated or impervious ground, it begins to flow over land downhill. The runoff may flow over bare soil and deposit sediment into rivers—which is not good for water quality. Only about a third of the precipitation that falls over land runs off into streams and rivers to be returned to the oceans. The other two-thirds is evaporated, transpired, or soaks into groundwater. Surface runoff is a resource that can also be diverted by humans for their own use.

Rivers serve a valuable role in the water cycle. People use the water for drinking-water supplies and irrigation water, to produce electricity, to flush away wastes, to transport merchandise, and to obtain food. Rivers are major aquatic landscapes for many types of plants and animals, and they help keep the aquifers underground full of water by discharging water downward through their streambeds.

Freshwater is also stored on the Earth's surface. Surface freshwater includes the streams, ponds, lakes, man-made reservoirs, and freshwater wetlands. Water is considered to be fresh when it contains less than 1,000 milligrams per liter of dissolved solids, most of which is often salt. The amount of water in rivers and lakes is always changing due to inflows and outflows, such as precipitation, overland runoff, or groundwater seepage. People often divert surface water for their own needs.

Infiltration is the downward movement of water from the land's surface into soil or porous rock. Anywhere in the world, a portion of the water that falls as rain or snow infiltrates into the subsurface soil and rock. Some of this water will remain in the shallow soil layer, where it will gradually move vertically and horizontally through the soil and subsurface material. Eventually, this water might enter a stream by seeping into the stream bank. Some of the water may infiltrate deeper into the ground, recharging groundwater aquifers. If the aquifer is shallow or porous enough to allow water to move freely through it, people can drill wells into the aquifer to retrieve the water. Water may travel long distances or remain in groundwater storage for long periods before returning to the surface or seeping into other water bodies, such as streams and oceans.

Large amounts of water are stored in the ground. The water still moves—although very slowly—and is a part of the water cycle. Most of the water in the ground comes from precipitation that infiltrates downward from the land's surface.

Groundwater is also a major contributor to flow in many streams and rivers and has a strong influence on river and wetland habitats for plants and animals. People have been using groundwater for thousands of years and continue to use it today, largely for drinking water and irrigation. Life on Earth depends on groundwater just as it does on surface water.

A spring is a water resource formed when the side of a hill, a valley bottom, or other excavation intersects a flowing body of groundwater at or below the local water table. A spring is the result of an aquifer being filled to the point that the water overflows onto the land surface. Springs range in size from intermittent seeps, which flow only after much rain, to huge pools with a flow of hundreds of millions of gallons (liters) per day.

Thermal springs are ordinary springs except that the water is warm—even hot in some springs. Many thermal springs occur in regions of recent volcanic activity and are fed by water heated by contact with hot rocks far below the surface. If the heated water reaches a large crevice that offers a path of less resistance, it may rise more quickly than it descended. Water that does not have time to cool before it emerges forms a thermal spring.

Community water supplies have their own water cycle within a cycle—based on the factors within the community that affect water uses and flow. Many local factors can have an impact on community water supplies, such as soil composition, buildings, pollution, surface water, type of terrain, amount of rainfall, land use, and population distribution and density. All of these factors can affect water quality and threaten to negatively impact a renewable resource to the point that it is no longer usable. For example, the impact of humans clearing the natural vegetation off the land can lead to erosion if the area receives large amounts of rainfall. Surface flow can erode bare soil, depositing it in streams, thereby polluting them.

In most urban communities, water is withdrawn from either a surface water body, like a lake, reservoir, or stream, or from an underground aquifer. This water is usually treated at a drinking-water treatment plant and distributed to individual homes, businesses, and industries through a huge network of underground pipes. Used water either flows into a drain and travels to a wastewater treatment plant through a network of sewer pipes or is deposited onto the ground. At the wastewater treatment plant, most pollutants are removed, and the treated water is released into a nearby surface water body, and the cycle begins again.

Every time water completes its cycle from vapor to liquid or solid and back to vapor again, its quality is renewed. Water quality can be damaged, however, by any number of pollutants in the air, on land, or from other water supplies. The amount of water available for use depends on its quality, and the availability of water dictates where people can live, build cities, and create industry.

Each time people use water, they change its quality by adding substances to it, such as municipal sewage, toxic chemicals, solvents, automotive oils, fertilizers, detergents, and pesticides. Some materials, even in small quantities, can damage water quality to the point that it becomes unusable. For example, according to the U.S. Environmental Protection Agency (EPA), a quart of motor oil has the potential to pollute as much as 250,000 gallons (946,353 liters) of water. Negatively affecting the water quality can make this renewable resource nonrenewable.

The Carbon Cycle

The carbon cycle is important because carbon is the basic structural material for all cell life. Carbon makes the soil productive, and plants healthy. The carbon cycle occurs with movement of carbon between the

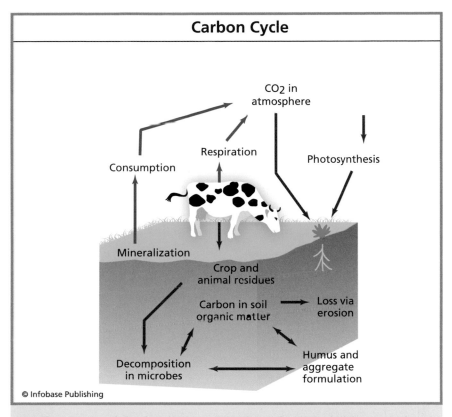

Carbon Cycle

Carbon is stored in the ocean, atmosphere, land, and living organisms. Additional carbon is added to the atmosphere through the burning of fossil fuels, which affects the natural carbon balance. Researchers are currently looking into ways to create carbon reservoirs to address serious issues, such as global warming.

atmosphere, the oceans, the land, and living organisms. Plants absorb carbon dioxide from the atmosphere during photosynthesis and then release some of it back into the atmosphere during cellular respiration.

Another major exchange of carbon dioxide happens between the oceans and the atmosphere. The dissolved carbon dioxide in the oceans is used by ocean plants in photosynthesis.

Carbon is also exchanged through the soil. Plant and animal residues decompose and form organic matter, which contains carbon. For plants to be able to use these nutrients, soil organisms break them down in a process called mineralization.

Animals give off carbon dioxide when they breathe. Some plants are eaten by grazing animals, which then return organic carbon to the soil as manure. Easily broken-down forms of carbon in manure and plant cells are released as carbon dioxide. Forms of carbon that are difficult to break down become stabilized in the soil as humus.

Atmospheric levels of carbon dioxide (CO_2) have risen from pre-industrial levels of 280 parts per million (ppm) to present levels of 375 ppm. Evidence suggests this observed rise in atmospheric CO_2 levels is due primarily to expanding use of fossil fuels for energy. Predictions of global energy use in the next century suggest a continued increase in carbon **emissions** and rising concentrations of CO_2 in the atmosphere unless major changes are made in the way we produce and use energy—in particular, how carbon use is managed.

One way to manage carbon dioxide levels is to use energy more efficiently to reduce the need for fossil fuel combustion. Another way is to increase the use of low-carbon and carbon-free fuels and technologies (nuclear power and renewable sources such as solar energy, wind power, and biomass fuels). Both approaches are supported by the U.S. Department of Energy (DOE). The third and newest way to manage carbon is through carbon sequestration.

Carbon sequestration is a process for the long-term storage of carbon in the terrestrial biosphere, underground, or in the oceans so that the buildup of carbon dioxide—the principal greenhouse gas—in the atmosphere will be reduced or slowed. In some cases, this is accomplished by maintaining or enhancing natural processes; in other cases, novel techniques are developed to dispose of carbon. DOE's Office of Science is focusing its efforts on several carbon sequestration options:

- Sequestering carbon in underground geologic repositories.
- Identifying ways to enhance carbon sequestration of the terrestrial biosphere through CO_2 removal from the

atmosphere by vegetation and storage in biomass and soils.

• Enhancing the net oceanic uptake from the atmosphere by fertilization of phytoplankton with nutrients and injecting CO_2 to ocean depths greater than 3,280 feet (1,000 m).

• Sequencing the genomes of microbes that produce fuels (such as methane and hydrogen or those that aid in carbon sequestration) to evaluate their potential to produce methane or hydrogen from either fossil fuels or other carbon sources, including biomass or even some waste products.

According to the DOE, understanding how these techniques perform, may enable us to enhance the ongoing natural processes. Developing innovative new processes may add powerful new measures to carbon management options.

The Nitrogen Cycle

The nitrogen cycle is the process by which the nitrogen in the atmosphere enters the soil and becomes part of living organisms, before returning to the atmosphere. Nitrogen makes up 78% of the Earth's atmosphere, but this nitrogen must be converted from a gas into a chemically usable form before living organisms can use it. This transformation takes place through the nitrogen cycle and transforms the nitrogen gas into ammonia or nitrates.

Most of the nitrogen conversion process is done biologically by free-living, nitrogen-fixing bacteria; bacteria living on the roots of plants; and through certain algae and lichens.

Nitrogen that has been converted to ammonia and nitrates is used directly by plants and is absorbed in their tissues as plant proteins. The nitrogen then passes from the plants to herbivores (plant-eating animals) and then to carnivores (meat-eating animals).

When plants and animals die, the nitrogen compounds are broken down by decomposing into ammonia. Plants then use some of this ammonia while the rest is either dissolved or held in the soil. Microorganisms then go to work on the ammonia in the soil and create nitrates in a process called nitrification. Nitrates can be stored in humus or washed from the soil and carried away to streams and lakes. Nitrates may also be converted and returned to the atmosphere by a process called dentrification.

The nitrogen cycle is important because plants need nitrogen to grow, develop, and produce seeds. The main source of nitrogen in soil is from organic matter (humus). Bacteria that live in the soil convert organic forms of nitrogen to inorganic forms that plants can use. Plant roots then take up nitrogen. When the plant dies, it decays and becomes part of the organic matter in the soil. The land must be well-managed or nitrogen can be washed out of the soil, which then negatively impacts the growth of plants.

AQUATIC AND ATMOSPHERIC RESOURCES

The ocean is the source of many resources, from petroleum reserves to ores mined from its depths to mineral salts used in a bath. Multitudes of seashells are used for decorative purposes. The oceans also provide a wide array of food. Vast amounts of mineral resources, as well as energy and construction resources, lie within the oceans.

People have always recognized the importance of coastal areas. Remnants of shells and bones left by ancient civilizations illustrate how life long ago depended on resources from the oceans. Along with providing for the dietary needs of ancient peoples, the oceans also provided the raw materials needed for shelter, transportation, economic exchange, and social needs. This is why so many major settlements are located near, or have access via river to, the ocean.

Food Resources

Animals and plants are a major marine resource. According to the National Oceanic and Atmospheric Administration and the U.S. Environmental Protection Agency, fish and shellfish, high in protein and other essential vitamins, provide 60% of the world's population

Fishing is a huge business and source of food. These shrimp fishermen at Beaufort, North Carolina, are sorting the catch brought in by large nets. *(Photo by National Oceanic and Atmospheric Administration, Fisheries Collection)*

with more than 40% of their annual protein. About 200 billion pounds (90,718,474,000 kilograms) of fish and shellfish are caught each year. More than one billion people receive their entire annual supply of protein from the sea. Although marine plants only provide 1% of our food—compared to 80% from land plants—marine plants are currently being used in bakery and dairy products, soft drinks, and industrial applications, such as tire manufacturing (because of the colloidal and gelling compounds that exist in seaweed).

Carrageenan and *alginate* are ingredients in many products. Carrageenans are compounds extracted from algae that are used to stabilize and gel food and pharmaceuticals. Brown algae contains alginates that make foods thicker and creamier and add to their shelf life. They are used to prevent ice crystals from forming in ice cream. Alginates and carrageenans are often used in puddings and milkshakes. The color additive *beta-carotene* often comes from green algae.

Marine **aquaculture**—also called *mariculture*—is the cultivation of aquatic organisms, such as fish, shellfish, algae, and other aquatic plants. Examples include raising catfish in freshwater ponds, farming salmon in net pens set out in a bay, trout farming, and even "growing" cultured pearls from oysters. Tuna farming is important in Australia.

According to scientists at the U.S. Department of Agriculture, aquaculture is the fastest growing sector of U.S. agriculture, as well as for the rest of the world. Many people see aquaculture as a solution to the problems caused by years of overfishing certain areas of the oceans, which has resulted in declining fish resources.

Fish farming is the main form of aquaculture. This is an operation where fish are raised in tanks or other types of enclosures, such as ponds. The fish are used mainly for food but are also used to "seed" sportfishing areas (meaning that fish are supplied to lakes and rivers for people to catch).

Some fish are raised in cages in existing water resources, such as streams and lakes. This system has many advantages; many different types of fish can be raised, and it can be done in the same areas where sportfishing occurs. Disadvantages include the unintentional spread of disease or other contaminants to wild fish populations. Fish that are used to stock lakes and rivers, such as trout, are usually raised from eggs to fingerlings (small fish) in long, shallow concrete tanks fed with fresh stream water and then released into lakes and rivers.

Fish farming can raise many species, such as salmon, catfish, tilapia, cod, and trout. Aquaculture is being monitored to look for drawbacks or problems. One of the largest problems is that it requires a lot of water—nearly a million gallons (3,785,412 l) of water per acre. Because of this, scientists have developed ways to recycle the water.

Another issue that is being closely monitored is the potential for the spread of unwanted invasive species. Farmed fish species can escape into open water and compete with native species for limited resources. If an invasive species competes with a native species, it can damage the ecosystem of that area. Another issue is the possibility of diseases being spread by farmed fish species. Nevertheless, aquaculture could prove to be a significant resource to support growing populations in the years to come. In the future, marine plants—such as kelp—may also be a possible food source to feed growing populations.

Transportation

The ocean is one of Earth's biggest transportation corridors. Tankers and freighters are able to efficiently ship goods to ports and harbors around the world. Crude oil ships, product ships, chemical ships, bulk carriers, cable layers, general cargo ships, offshore supply vessels, ferries, gas and car carriers, tugboats, barges, and dredgers use oceans extensively for transportation.

The oceans and waterways also provide transportation for exploration, such as the navigation of major rivers to discover new areas—from the great explorers' sailing ships in the 1600s that came to America to boats today that navigate the Amazon River to reach uncharted territory.

Oceans also provide transportation avenues for the military. By serving as routes for naval ships, the waters can be protected and coastlines defended. Another business that relies on transportation passages on the oceans are cruise line ships. Millions of people enjoy sailing to world ports for recreation, relaxation, and tourism. In the Arctic, the broad expanses of snow and ice are used by dogsleds, snowmobiles, and other vehicles for transportation corridors between towns.

Aquatic Systems

Aquatic systems provide water for drinking, aquifers, surface water, groundwater, wetlands, and estuaries. Most of the Earth's water, located in the oceans, is too salty to drink. It is also too salty to use for farming or industry because the salt would kill most crops and would ruin most machinery.

Dogsleds are commonly used for transportation over the ground of the frozen Arctic regions. Although these dogs may look small, they are heavily insulated with two fur coats and have exceptional endurance in harsh conditions. *(Photo courtesy of National Oceanic and Atmospheric Administration)*

Because only a small percentage of the water on Earth is fresh, it is a critical resource for the survival of life. In the United States, about 4% of the landmass is covered by surface water. The United States has 60,000 community water supply systems, but only 20% of these use surface water as their primary source. Groundwater is the primary source of water for 80% of U.S. communities (comprising nearly half of the U.S. population). According to the U.S. Environmental Protection Agency, each American uses about 50 gallons (189 l) of water each day. In highly populated areas, drinking water can become scarce (such as during a drought).

In 1974, Congress passed the Safe Drinking Water Act (SDWA), setting up a regulatory program among local, state, and federal agencies to help ensure safe drinking water in the United States. This act states that public water systems must provide water treatment, monitor drinking water to ensure proper quality, and provide public notification of containment problems. The Act establishes drinking-water standards for a variety of chemicals, metals, and pathogens. The SDWA protects drinking-water supplies through required treatment, testing, and reporting. It also requires protection of aquifers, groundwater, and surface water sources for drinking-water supplies.

Drinking water is treated because when it rains or snows, the water picks up dust, smoke, and other particles in the air. Runoff water dissolves minerals and carries small particles of soil. Streams can carry sediment, human-made pollutants, and other materials. Once people use water, it picks up even more pollutants and impurities. The need for a supply of clean water requires water treatment methods that make it safe and healthy to use.

Seawater is a readily available and plentiful resource. Because of its salinity, however, seawater is unsuitable for drinking, and it must be treated before it can be used. Desalination is an expensive process that is mainly used in arid and coastal areas where water is so scarce that the need for survival makes the process cost effective. As freshwater supplies become tighter, desalination may become more cost effective and practical to use. For example, some desalination plants have been built in Southern California to meet the high water demands that exist there.

An aquifer is an underground layer of water-bearing permeable rock or unconsolidated materials (gravel, sand, silt, or clay) from which groundwater can be usefully extracted by using a water well. Groundwater is recharged from, and eventually flows to, the surface naturally. Natural discharge occurs at springs and seeps and can also form oases or **swamps**.

Deep groundwater can take a long time to complete its natural cycle and is replenished by surface water from precipitation, streams, and

A diverse amount of life exists in the intertidal zones of the oceans. These crabs live along the coast of Fernandina Island, Galapagos Islands, Ecuador. Water pollution has a disastrous effect on fragile ocean life, making proper management and conservation practices critical to the survival of the delicate ecosystems. *(Photo courtesy National Oceanic and Atmospheric Administration; photo by Rosalind Cohen, NODC, NOA, Small World Collection)*

rivers when this recharge reaches the water table. It is estimated that the volume of groundwater is 50 times that of surface freshwater. Only the Earth's ice caps and glaciers are larger reservoirs of freshwater.

Ecosystems and Biodiversity

Aquatic ecosystems exist in oceans, lakes, rivers and streams, estuaries, and wetlands. The oceans contain much of the Earth's plant and animal life. Lakes are resources for water storage, flood control, recreation,

Many coastal regions are inhabited by different species of animals. The seals in this photo live along the coast, where they catch fish from the ocean as a food source. Human interference and pollution have threatened wildlife populations in many coastal areas of the world. *(Photo courtesy of National Oceanic and Atmospheric Administration, NOAA Research-Environmental Technology Laboratory, NOAA's Small World Collection)*

and fisheries. Rivers and streams also support wide varieties of life. Estuaries function as spawning grounds and preserves for many animal species, such as shellfish. They are also important for commercial fishing and recreational aquifers. Wetlands are lands that are periodically covered with water. The true importance of wetlands is just now being realized. They keep surface waters clean by filtering out sediment and trapping pollutants. Coastal wetlands cushion drier lands from the

Coastal and wetland areas provide homes for diverse species of waterfowl. These birds are blue-footed boobies (*Sula nebouxii*), found along the coast of Espanola Island, Galapagos Islands, Ecuador. Human misuse of the environment and the effects of pollution can have disastrous effects on wildlife populations. *(Photo courtesy of National Oceanic and Atmospheric Administration; photo by Rosalind Cohen, Small World Collection)*

full impact of storms. They help control floods by temporarily storing runoff waters. Coastal wetlands also provide habitat for fish, shellfish, waterfowl, and mammals. Coastal estuaries and marshes are among the most productive areas in the world, providing organic matter for the base of the food chain and the spawning grounds for fisheries. They provide billions of dollars of food sources each year.

There are many types of aquatic habitats. The major determinant of aquatic habitats is the amount of dissolved oxygen in the water. Cold, fast-running mountain streams that run over rocks and splash down slopes dissolve high amounts of oxygen, making them perfect habitats for fish like trout, which require high levels of oxygen. As waters level out and become more still, they absorb heat from the sun and lose oxygen content. Trout may not be able to survive in them, but other fish like bass, crappie, and bluegill thrive there. If water gets too warm and oxygen content gets lower, then fish like carp and suckers move in.

Plant life also thrives around lakes and streams. The immediate environment around a body of water is known as a riparian area because it supports so much plant life. On public waterways, riparian areas are carefully managed to keep water ecosystems balanced.

Wetland areas have their own unique habitats. They are such complex areas that hundreds of species of plants and animals live there. They are nurseries for many species of animals and provide food to nourish the most productive fishing beds. According to experts at the U.S. Fish and Wildlife Service, more than half of all rare and endangered animal species are either located in wetland areas or are dependent on them.

Biodiversity has an enormous impact on determining water quality. Diverse natural ecosystems provide important ecological services. They maintain hydrological cycles, regulate climate, contribute to the processes of soil formation and maturation, store and recycle essential nutrients, and absorb and break down pollutants.

Mineral Resources

Salt and other minerals are ocean resources. When seawater evaporates, salt is left. Seawater can be piped into shallow basins and allowed to evaporate. The different chemicals in the water crystallize at different times. Unwanted chemicals are removed by transferring the water from one basin to another as it evaporates. After the water has evaporated, what remains is almost pure sodium chloride—also called table salt. Extraction of salt as a resource is the most practical in hot, dry climates where the sun provides the energy to evaporate the water. Magnesium and bromine are also produced from sea salt.

In the 1950s, people began to mine the ocean floor for diamonds, gold, silver, metal ores like manganese nodules, and gravel mines. Diamonds are found in greater numbers in the ocean than on land but are much harder to mine. When diamonds are mined, the ocean floor is dredged to bring sediment up to the boat where it is then sifted to trap valuable gems.

Metal compounds, gravels, sands, and gas hydrates are mined in the ocean. Mining of manganese nodules containing nickel, copper, and cobalt began in the 1960s. At the present time, manganese nodules are expensive to mine. As new technology is developed, scientists expect to be able to tap into this mineral resource.

There are drawbacks to mining, however. It can be devastating to natural ecosystems. Dredging of any kind pulls up the ocean floor, resulting in widespread destruction of marine animal habitats as well as wiping out vast numbers of fish and invertebrates. When the ocean floor is mined, a cloud of sediment rises up in the water, interfering with photosynthetic processes of phytoplankton and other marine life in addition to introducing heavy metals into the food chain.

Petroleum and Natural Gas

Petroleum is formed when billions of dead single-celled marine creatures are buried under layers of undersea sediments for millions of years. The creatures' remains gradually changed into oil and gas. Because of this, much of the world's petroleum is produced from undersea wells.

Oil companies set up huge drilling rigs in coastal waters. Several wells can be drilled from each rig. Common drilling locations include the Gulf of Mexico, the North Sea, the Persian Gulf, and along the coasts of Southern California and Venezuela. Setting up platforms and drilling is expensive and dangerous work, especially in the stormy waters found in the North Sea. Oil spills sometimes result as tankers transfer the petroleum from well to refinery. These spills damage beaches and kill marine life.

Power Generation

The oceans can provide nonpolluting, renewable energy resources. The winds, waves, **tides**, and heat energy in ocean water can all be harnessed to generate electrical power. Winds along the coasts are usually steady and reliable because the sun heats the land and sea unevenly. The sea-coast is a good place for building wind-powered generators, which are a proven method for bringing electricity to many places. Power generation is discussed in more detail in Chapter 4.

Climate Buffering and Oxygen Production

The ocean also serves as a climatic buffer. It is an integral component of the world's climate due to its capacity to collect, drive, and mix water and heat. The ocean and the atmosphere work together to form complex weather phenomena. The ocean could also buffer events like the greenhouse effect or **global warming** by holding the heat energy for long periods of time and releasing it at a later date. The many chemical cycles that occur between the ocean and the atmosphere also influence the climate by controlling the amount of radiation that is released into ecosystems and the environment. The temperature of the ocean controls the climate in the lower part of the atmosphere, so for most areas of the Earth, the ocean temperature is directly responsible for the air temperature.

The ocean buffers the climate by transporting heat through ocean currents that travel across huge basins. This action cools the tropics and warms the higher latitudes. Air temperatures worldwide are regulated by the circulation of heat by the oceans. The ocean stores heat in the upper 2 meters (6.6 feet) of the photic zone. This is possible because seawater has a very high density and specific heat and can store vast quantities of energy in the form of heat. The ocean can then buffer changes in temperature by storing and releasing heat. Evaporation cools ocean water, which cools the atmosphere. It is most noticeable near the equator, and the effect decreases closer to the poles.

Phytoplankton account for 90% of the world's oxygen production because water covers more than 70% of the Earth, and phytoplankton are abundant in the photic zone of the surface layers. Some of the oxygen produced by phytoplankton is absorbed by the ocean, but most flows into the atmosphere where it becomes available for oxygen-dependent life-forms.

Sand and Gravel

Sand and gravel resources from the ocean provide enormous amounts of construction materials. Sand and gravel play an important role in the quality of life for all Americans. In the 1700s, sand was used to make plaster, bricks, and mortar (the cement that holds bricks in place). Gravel was used for making concrete and as a pavement for early roads.

Today, sand and gravel are dredged from the bottom of lakes and rivers and moved by barge to a processing plant and storage site. Sand is also dredged from shallow ocean waters. Sand and gravel quarries are present at the sites of ancient lakebeds and on deposits of land that were once covered by water. Sand and gravel are used in many construction materials. For example, asphalt pavement is made up of more than 90% sand and gravel, and concrete is more than 80% sand and gravel. Nearly 20,000 tons of sand, gravel, and crushed rock are needed to build 1 mile (0.6 km) of a four-lane highway, and an average of 120 tons are required to build a new house in the United States. Most of this goes into concrete for foundations; basement walls and floors; bricks; blocks; and pavement for driveways, sidewalks, and parking areas.

Sand and silt (material smaller than sand grains) are also used as fillers in many products people use every day, such as toothpaste, medicines, rubber, and cardboard. In fact, according to the U.S. Minerals Management Service, every American uses an average of 21,000 pounds (9,525 kg) of sand and silt products each year.

Tourism

Marine recreation is on the rise. People crowd to beaches and coastal areas to enjoy fishing, boating, swimming, scuba diving, shell collecting, sailing, surfing, wave running, and many other activities. The ocean provides a deep aesthetic joy that many people find enriches their lives. Millions of tourists each year choose coastal vacation destinations to enjoy the beauty of ocean resources. Tourism and recreation will be looked at in more detail in Chapter 6.

Ocean environments are valued as destinations for tourism and recreation. Outrigger sailing (above) is a popular tourist activity in Hawaii. *(Photo courtesy of Nature's Images)*

Ozone

As outlined previously, ozone in the stratosphere is a valuable natural resource because it protects life on Earth from the sun's harmful ultraviolet (UV) rays. Impacts to this natural shield expose humans to unhealthy radiation levels. This is one resource that must be carefully managed in order to benefit from its presence.

For the most part—with the exception of petroleum, natural gas, and other mineral deposits—resources from the water and atmosphere are renewable. Renewability, however, is closely tied to the activities of humans and the manner in which the environment is cared for. If water and air sources become polluted, they may cease to function as useful natural resources. Because the atmospheric and water systems are so dynamic and fragile, great care must be taken when exploiting these natural resources. We have a responsibility to use them wisely and preserve them globally. In fact, the future of the Earth is tightly bound to the health of the oceans and atmosphere.

DEVELOPMENT OF OCEAN AND ATMOSPHERIC RESOURCES

This chapter will focus on how development of oceanic and atmospheric resources has benefited society, as well as how these developments have impacted natural resources and the environment. This chapter will focus on ocean energy, hydroelectric power, geothermal resources, wind energy, and air-quality issues.

OCEAN ENERGY

There are many sources of energy connected to the ocean—radiant energy from the sun; wind energy, manifested by the reliable and constant coastal breezes; constantly moving waves; and rising and falling tides. The oceans can provide nonpolluting, renewable energy resources. The winds, waves, tides, and heat energy in ocean water can all be harnessed to generate electrical power.

The world's oceans may someday provide enough energy to power homes, businesses, and other buildings. Places—such as several locations in California—are beginning to utilize this tremendous natural resource for energy. There are three basic ways to tap the ocean itself for energy: (1) energy from the ocean's waves, (2) high and low tides, and (3) temperature differences. The first two methods are classified as mechanical energy; the third is classified as thermal energy.

In addition to this renewable power, there is also nonrenewable energy associated with the oceans. Below the ocean, buried in the seabed, there are enormous deposits of petroleum and natural gas. There are also huge deposits of frozen crystals filled with methane—an energy-rich gas.

Scientists believe that the oceans and the land beneath them could provide all of the energy the world needs for years to come. Today, according to the U.S. Department of Energy, more than a quarter of the oil and gas produced in the United States comes from offshore areas. U.S. territory actually extends 200 miles (322 km) into the water from the coastline. This underwater area encompasses an area larger than the country itself, about 3.9 billion acres. (For comparison, the land area of the country includes only 2.3 billion acres.) This area is referred to as the exclusive economic zone (EEZ). The Minerals Management Service of the U.S. Department of the Interior is responsible for protecting and developing the natural resources it contains.

Petroleum and Natural Gas

Petroleum and natural gas deposits are found in sedimentary rock basins where tiny sea plants and animals died millions of years ago. With the proper temperature and pressure, the remains of these plants and animals eventually turned into hydrocarbons such as oil and gas, which are made mostly of hydrogen and carbon. These hydrocarbons flowed into empty spaces in the surrounding rocks, called traps. Finally, an oil-soaked rock—similar to a wet sponge—was formed. Over time, the traps were covered with a layer of solid rock, or a seal of salt or clay, that created a reservoir that kept the oil and gas from escaping to the surface.

Currently, 30 basins in the EEZ have been found that could contain enormous oil and gas deposits. Some of these basins have been explored and are producing oil and gas now. Scientists estimate that 30% of U.S. gas and oil reserves are in these offshore basins.

The first offshore drilling was begun in 1897 from a pier in California. Early drilling was limited to areas where the water was less than 300 feet (91 m) deep, but modern drilling rigs can now operate to depths of a mile (1.6 km) or more. Some drilling platforms stand on stilt-like legs that are embedded in the ocean floor. These huge platforms hold all the drilling equipment, as well as housing and storage areas for the work crews. Once the wells have been drilled, the platforms also hold the production equipment.

Floating platforms are used for drilling in deeper waters. These self-propelled vessels are anchored to the ocean bottom with huge cables. Once the wells have been drilled from these platforms, the production equipment is lowered to the ocean floor and sealed to the well casing to prevent leakage. Wells have been drilled in 10,000 feet (3,048 m) of water using these floating rigs.

During every phase of development and production, precautions are taken to prevent pollution, spills, and significant changes to the ocean environment. All aspects of the operation, from waste disposal to hurricane safety measures, are regulated.

Today, there are more than 4,000 platforms in the Gulf of Mexico and off the coasts of California and Alaska, servicing thousands of wells. Offshore production supplies approximately 27% of the nation's natural gas and 20% of its oil. Most of the active wells and proven reserves are in the Gulf of Mexico. There is also believed to be significant petroleum in the Beaufort Sea, off Alaska, as well as significant natural gas in the Eastern Gulf of Mexico and off the Atlantic Coast.

There are also alternate uses of existing oil and gas platforms. The passage of the Energy Policy Act of 2005 gave the Minerals Management Service (MMS) of the U.S. government jurisdiction over other projects that make alternate use of existing oil and natural gas platforms in federal waters. Offshore oil and gas structures can remain in place after oil and gas activities have stopped and be used for other energy and marine-related activities. This allows the life span of facilities to be extended for non-oil-and-gas purposes before being removed. Alternate uses of existing facilities may include offshore aquaculture, research, education, recreation, support for other offshore operations and facilities, and telecommunication facilities.

Methane Hydrates

Methane is an energy-rich gas and is the main component of natural gas. According to the U.S. Minerals Management Service, a reserve of methane buried in the sediments of the ocean floor is so huge that scientists believe there could be enough to fuel the entire world. Bacteria break down the remains of the sea animals and plants, and as they do, they produce methane gas (which is almost always a by-product of organic decay). The methane gas then dissolves under the enormous pressures and cold temperatures at the bottom of the ocean. The molecules of methane become locked in an enclosure of water molecules to form crystals. These crystals resemble ice. In some places, a solid layer of crystals—called methane hydrate—extends from the seafloor down hundreds of yards (m).

In addition to the methane trapped in crystals, scientists think that huge deposits of free methane gas are trapped beneath the hydrate layer. Hydrates are believed to be the richest reservoirs of methane known to exist. Researchers estimate that there is more carbon trapped in hydrates than in all the fossil fuels—which represents an enormous amount of energy.

Some of this methane is trapped in polar ice, but most is located in the waters off the East and West coasts of the United Sates, as well as Alaska. In fact, one deposit off the coast of North Carolina holds enough methane to supply all the needs of the United States for 100 years. The challenge that experts face is finding ways to recover this methane safely and economically. Most of the hydrates are at depths of 3,281 to 9,842 feet (1,000 to 3,000 m). Researchers think that it may be possible to free the methane from the crystals by reducing the pressure on them.

One possible drawback, however, is that recovery efforts might cause an increase in methane escaping into the atmosphere. Because methane is a greenhouse gas, scientists think that methane from ocean hydrates may have a negative impact on global climate. Therefore, any wide-scale attempts to harvest methane from ocean hydrates will have to take into account the environmental impacts to the ocean floor and the atmosphere. Much research must be done before methane hydrate becomes a usable energy source for the future.

Solar Energy

According to experts at the Minerals Management Service, the sun radiates more energy in one second than the world has used since time began. Only a small portion of this energy strikes the Earth—one part in two billion. Yet, this amount of energy is enough to meet the world's needs, if it could be harnessed. About 15% of the radiant energy that reaches the Earth is reflected back into space. Another 30% is used to evaporate water, which is lifted into the atmosphere to produce rainfall. Plants, landmasses, and the oceans also absorb the radiant energy.

Most of the ocean's energy comes from the sun. Only the tides—which are caused by the gravitational energy of the moon—and the geothermal energy under the oceans are not solar powered. Ocean currents, waves, and winds all are a result of the sun's radiant energy. Solar energy can also be used to produce electricity with photovoltaics.

Solar energy technologies that are potentially suitable for use in offshore ocean environments include concentrating solar power (CSP) technology and photonic technology. CSP is a thermal solar technology that concentrates the sun's rays in order to heat fluids or solids. This heat is then used to drive steam turbines or other devices to generate power. Photonic technologies convert the sun's radiant energy directly to electricity or other useful forms of energy. Selection of the appropriate solar technology for a given situation depends in part on the intended use of the energy to be generated. CSP technologies might be more appropriate for generating and delivering electricity to shore, while photonic technology might be more appropriate for generation of electricity to be used on-site.

All CSP technological approaches and PV systems require large areas for solar radiation collection when they are used to produce electricity at the multi-megawatt scale. On the outer continental shelf (OCS), this large surface area array of solar collectors would need to be supported on some type of offshore floating or fixed structures. The downfall to having these structures, however, is that they will interfere with commercial and recreational fishing and also with recreational boating, surfing, and diving. It will also disturb ecosystems by blocking sunlight from the water's surface.

Other potential environmental impacts from CSP systems include accidental or emergency releases of toxic chemicals that may be used in the heat transfer systems; interference with aircraft operations if reflected light beams become misdirected into aircraft pathways; ecosystem disturbances from discharges related to the maintenance of cooling water systems; discharges related to the operation and maintenance of recycled steam systems; and ecosystem disturbances from construction, operation, and maintenance of both the solar energy conversion systems and the systems that transport electricity to onshore customers. Structures used for both CSP and photonic technologies in offshore applications would also have visual impacts in some areas.

Wind Energy

Wind is air in motion. It is produced by the uneven heating of the Earth's surface by the sun. Since the Earth's surface is made of various land and water formations, it absorbs the sun's radiation unevenly. When the sun is shining during the day, the air over landmasses heats more quickly than the air over water. The warm air over the land expands and rises, while the heavier, cooler air over the water moves in to take its place, creating local winds. At night, the winds are reversed because the air over land cools more rapidly than the air over water. Similarly, the large atmospheric winds that circle the Earth are created because the surface air near the equator is warmed more by the sun than the air over the North and South poles.

Wind energy is mainly used to generate electricity. Windmills work by slowing down the speed of the wind. The wind flows over the airfoil-shaped blades causing lift, like the effect it has on airplane wings, causing them to turn. The blades are connected to a driveshaft that turns an electric generator to produce electricity. Wind turbines are now being installed on offshore oil and gas platforms in many areas to generate power to operate the equipment.

Wind systems are created by the uneven heating of land and water surfaces. These predominant winds can be predicted, and energy technologies can be designed to make use of wind resources.

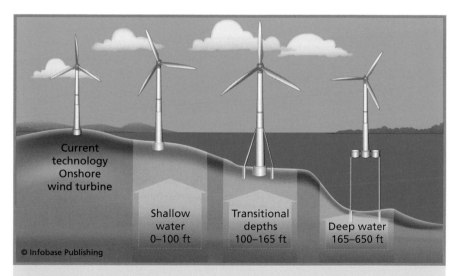

Deep-water wind turbines can be developed to take advantage of ocean breezes. They can be located at depths up to 650 feet (200 m).

This is the Arklow Bank, Ireland Offshore Wind Farm, located about 6 miles (10 km) off the coast of Arklow, Ireland. This wind park is the world's first commercial application of offshore wind turbines that is more than 3 megawatts in size, and Ireland's first offshore wind facility. *(Photo courtesy of National Oceanic and Atmospheric Administration)*

For wind machines to be economical, there must be winds that blow consistently above 10 to 14 miles (16 to 23 km) per hour. Many offshore areas have ideal wind conditions for wind machines. Denmark and the United Kingdom have installed large offshore wind parks to take advantage of the consistent winds. Several offshore parks are planned for the United States in the near future, including one in Nantucket **Sound** and one off Long Island, New York.

Wave Energy

Waves are caused by the wind blowing over the surface of the ocean. In many areas of the world, the wind blows with enough consistency and force to provide continuous waves. There is an enormous amount of energy contained in the ocean waves. For example, the total power of waves breaking on the world's coastlines is estimated at 2 to 3 million megawatts. Scientists believe that the west coasts of the United States and Europe and the coasts of Japan and New Zealand are good sites for harnessing wave energy.

One way to harness this energy is to bend, or focus, the waves into a narrow channel, increasing their power and size. The waves can then be channeled into a catch basin, like tidal plants, or used directly to spin turbines. There are not any big commercial wave energy plants yet, but there are a few small ones. Small, onshore sites have the best potential for the immediate future, especially if they can also be used to protect beaches and harbors. They could produce enough energy to power local communities. Japan, which must import almost all of its fuel, has an active wave-energy program.

Another way to harness wave energy is with an oscillating water column (OWC) that generates electricity from the wave-driven rise and fall of water in a cylindrical shaft or pipe. The rising and falling water drives air into and out of the top of the shaft, powering an air-driven turbine. In Norway, a demonstration tower that is built into a cliff produces electricity very economically using this method. The wail of the fast-spinning turbines, however, is very loud and can be heard from far away, making the tower an annoyance for populated areas.

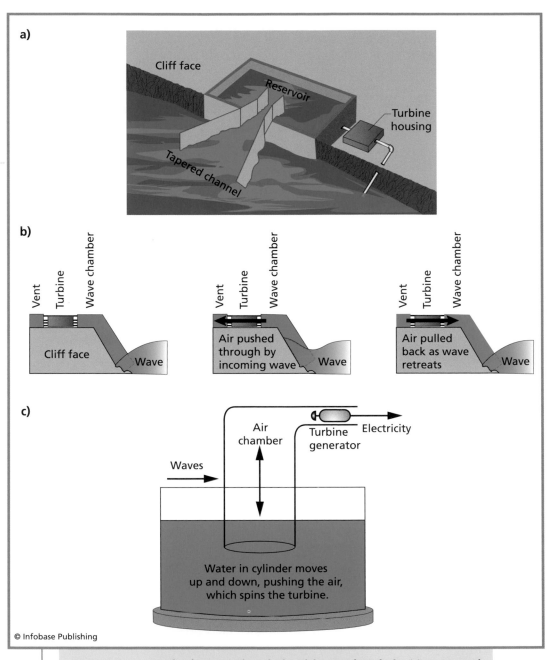

Wave energy can be harnessed and electricity produced via (a) a tapered channel and reservoir, (b) an oscillating water column (OWC), or (c) float devices.

This is an attenuator wave energy device. Attenuators are long, multi-segmented floating structures oriented parallel to the direction of the waves. The differing height of waves along the length of the device causes flexing where the segments connect. This flexing is connected to hydraulic pumps or other energy converters. *(Photo courtesy of National Oceanic and Atmospheric Administration)*

Float devices can generate electricity from the bobbing action of a floating object. The object can be mounted on a floating raft or on a device fixed on the ocean floor. These types of devices can power lights and whistles on buoys.

Ocean Thermal Energy Conversion (OTEC)

The energy from the sun heats the surface water of the ocean. In tropical regions, the surface water can be 40 or more degrees warmer than the deep water. Scientists at the World Energy Council believe that this temperature difference can be used to produce electricity. Ocean thermal energy conversion (OTEC) has the potential to produce more energy than tidal, wave, and wind energy combined.

The OTEC systems can be open or closed. In a closed system, an evaporator turns warm surface water into steam under pressure. This steam then spins a turbine generator to produce electricity. Water pumps bring cold deep water through pipes to a condenser on the surface. The cold water condenses the steam, and the closed cycle begins again. In an open system, the steam is turned into freshwater, and new surface water is added to the system. A transmission cable carries the electricity to the shore.

The OTEC systems must have a temperature difference of about 77°F (25°C) in order to successfully operate. Because of this, OTEC's use is limited to tropical regions where the surface waters are very warm and there is deep cold water. Hawaii, with its tropical climate, has been experimenting with OTEC systems since the 1970s.

Today there are many experimental OTEC plants, but no large operations. There are many challenges to widespread use. The OTEC systems are not very energy efficient. Pumping the water is a giant engineering challenge. In addition, the electricity must be transported to land. Scientists at the National Renewable Energy Laboratory project it will be 10 to 20 years before the technology is available to produce and transmit electricity economically from OTEC systems.

Tidal Energy

The tides rise and fall in constant cycles. Tides are changes in the level of the oceans caused by the gravitational pull of the moon and sun, and the rotation of the Earth. Nearshore water levels can vary up to 40 feet (12 m), depending on the season and local factors. Only about 20 locations, however, have good inlets and a large enough tidal range—about 10 feet (3 m)—to produce energy economically.

The generation of electricity from tides is similar to hydroelectric generation, except that tidal water flows in two directions. The simplest generating system for tidal plants involves a dam, known as a barrage, across an inlet. Sluice gates on the barrage allow the tidal basin to fill on the incoming high tides and to empty through the turbine system on the outgoing tide, known as the ebb tide. Flood-generating systems that generate power from the incoming tide are possible, but are less favored than ebb-generating systems. Two-way generation systems, which generate electricity on both the incoming and ebb rides, are also possible.

Tidal turbines are a new technology that can be used in many areas. Tidal turbines are basically wind turbines that can be located wherever there is strong tidal flow, as well as in river estuaries. There are both advantages and disadvantages to using tidal turbines. Tidal turbines must be engineered to be much stronger than the land-based wind turbines, because water is about 800 times denser than air. To be sturdier, they will have to be heavier, which makes them more expensive. The positive side is that these machines will be able to capture larger quantities of energy, making them more efficient.

Ocean Current Energy

Ocean waters are constantly on the move. Ocean currents flow in complex patterns affected by the wind, water salinity and temperature, topography of the ocean floor, and the Earth's rotation. The ocean currents are driven by wind and solar heating of the waters near the equator, though some ocean currents result from density and salinity variations of water. These currents are relatively constant and flow in one direction only, in contrast to the tidal currents closer to shore. Some examples of significant ocean currents are the Gulf Stream, the Florida **Straits** Current, and the California Current.

Ocean currents carry a huge amount of energy because water is very dense. For example, for the same surface area, water that is moving 12 miles (19 km) per hour (mph) exerts about the same amount of force as a constant 110-mph (177 km/hr) wind. Scientists believe ocean currents contain an enormous amount of energy that can be captured and converted to a usable form. For example, it has been estimated that taking just one-one thousandth of the available energy from the Gulf Stream would supply the state of Florida with 35% of its electrical needs.

The United States, Japan, China, and some European Union countries are pursuing ocean current energy. However, marine current energy is still at an early stage of development. Scientists are focusing on extracting energy from ocean currents by using submerged water turbines that are similar to wind turbines. These turbines would have rotor blades, a generator for converting the rotational energy into electricity, and a means of transporting the electrical current to shore for incorporation into the electrical grid.

For ocean current energy to be utilized successfully at a commercial scale, a number of potential technical challenges need to be addressed, such as controlling bubble formation, preventing marine growth buildup on the machines, building low-maintenance/high-reliability equipment, and creating resistance to corrosion from ocean water.

HYDROELECTRIC POWER

Moving water from streams and rivers that run down to the ocean can be used to do work. For hundreds of years, moving water was used to turn wooden wheels that were attached to grinding wheels to grind (or mill) flour or corn. Water can either go over the top of the wheel or the wheel can be placed in the moving river. Today, moving water can also be used to make electricity.

Hydro means "water." *Hydroelectric* refers to making electricity from waterpower. Hydroelectric power uses the kinetic energy of moving water to make electricity. Dams can be built to stop the flow of a river. Water behind a dam often forms a reservoir. Dams are also built across larger rivers without creating a reservoir. The river is simply routed through a hydroelectric power plant or powerhouse.

According to the U.S. Department of Energy, hydroelectric power is one of the largest producers of electricity in the United States. Waterpower supplies about 10% of the entire electricity that is used. In states with high mountains and lots of rivers, even more electricity can be made by hydropower. Today, the state of Washington leads the nation in hydroelectric energy generation.

The technology of the modern-day dam has contributed greatly to the widespread generation of hydropower. The water behind the dam flows through the intake pipe and into another pipe called a penstock.

The water pushes against blades in a turbine, causing them to turn. The turbine spins a generator to produce electricity. The electricity can then travel over long-distance electric lines to homes, schools, factories, and businesses. Hydropower today can be found in the mountainous areas of states where there are lakes and rivers.

Reservoirs from dams serve several water needs. They provide storage for large supplies of water for industrial, commercial, and residential use. They also control floods and other natural disasters that can cause water pollution. They generate power and provide places for recreation. While building dams removes certain types of habitats, it also creates new habitats that support thousands of species of wildlife.

While dams provide significant supplies of energy, there are also some environmental drawbacks. Scientists have identified the following possible environmental impacts associated with the construction of dams:

- *River habitat upstream can be changed:* Sometimes dams can flood the area around them. Severe flooding can damage both river and terrestrial (land) habitats along riverbanks. These riparian habitats can have diverse, fragile ecosystems associated with them. Oftentimes, the construction of a dam reduces the species diversity in the area's ecosystem.
- *Changes in the downstream shape of the riverbed and banks:* When rivers flow into reservoirs, the sediment they carry is deposited in the reservoir. Over time, these sediments build up at the bottom. When water is released from the dam, the sediment gets left behind the dam, so the discharged water that runs downstream from the dam has less sediment. With less sediment in the water downstream, the water's power becomes very erosive and erodes both the riverbed and riverbanks. If too much of the sediment downstream is eroded, the fish habitat can be damaged. Eventually, the stream will erode deeper, which will reduce the animal and plant diversity.

Hoover Dam in Nevada is the structure holding back Lake Mead in this photograph. The dam is a major producer of electricity. *(Photo courtesy of Natural Resources Conservation Service, photo by Lynn Betts)*

- *Impact on water quality downstream:* The chemical and physical properties of the water can change as a result of being held in a reservoir. For example, turbidity, temperature, lack of oxygen, and lack of nutrients can become an issue. In addition, heavy metals and minerals can affect the water quality. All of these factors can negatively impact the diverse ecosystems downstream.
- *Reduced biodiversity:* Biodiversity can become reduced and river ecosystems fragmented. The presence of dams can also interrupt natural migrations of fish, such as those that travel upriver to spawn.

GEOTHERMAL RESOURCES

For every 328 feet (100 m) underground from the Earth's surface, the temperature of the rock increases about 5.4°F (3°C). This means that at a depth of 10,000 feet (3,048 m) below ground, the temperature of the rock is hot enough to boil water. Deep under the surface, water sometimes makes its way close to the hot rock and turns into boiling hot water or steam. The hot water can reach temperatures of more than 300°F (148°C)—which is hotter than boiling water (212°F or 100°C). It does not turn into steam until it comes in contact with the air.

When this hot water comes up through a crack in the Earth, it is called a **hot spring**. When it explodes into the air, it is a geyser. Millions of people from around the world have visited the hot springs and geysers in Yellowstone National Park.

People use geothermally heated hot water in swimming pools and in health spas. The hot water from below the ground can also be used to warm buildings for growing plants in greenhouses. It is also used to heat buildings during the winter by enabling hot water to run through insulated pipes. Hot water or steam from below ground can also be used to make electricity in a geothermal power plant. Some areas have enough steam and hot water to generate electricity. In order to obtain this energy, holes are drilled into the ground, and pipes are lowered into the hot water. The hot steam or water comes up through pipes from below ground.

A geothermal power plant is like a traditional power plant except that the water is heated into steam directly by the Earth (instead of by burning fuel) and goes into a special turbine. The steam makes the turbine blades spin, and the shaft from the turbine, which is connected to a generator, makes electricity. The steam gets cooled off in a cooling tower until it is water again. The cooled water can then be pumped back below ground to be reheated by the Earth. In areas with geothermal properties, this represents a clean, renewable energy source.

Because of its unique geological conditions, the country of Iceland heats many of its buildings and swimming pools with geothermal hot water. Iceland's capitol—Reykjavik—is heated extensively with

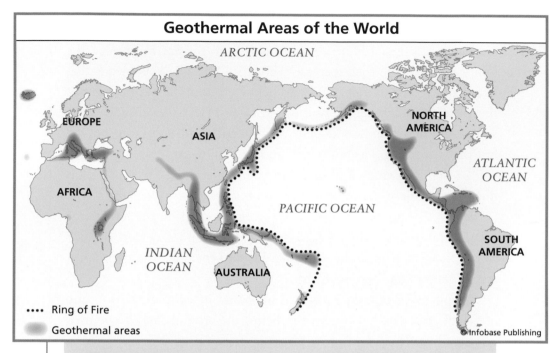

Geothermal Areas of the World

.... Ring of Fire

Geothermal areas

© Infobase Publishing

Geothermal areas are only located in certain areas around the world along plate boundaries, most notably along the Pacific Ring of Fire.

geothermal energy sources. Iceland has at least 25 active volcanoes and many hot springs and geysers.

WIND ENERGY

Just as wind energy over the oceans can be utilized, wind over land can also be used to generate renewable energy. This energy is mainly used to generate electricity. Today's wind machines are much more technologically advanced than the early windmills. Although they still use blades to collect the wind's kinetic energy, the blades today are made of fiberglass or other high-strength materials. Modern wind machines still have not solved the problem of what to do when the wind is not blowing, however. One solution is to use another type of generator at the utility site as a backup to pick up the load when there is no wind available. Small turbines are sometimes connected to diesel/electric generators or sometimes have a battery to store the extra energy they collect when the wind is blowing hard.

A typical horizontal wind machine is huge—it stands as tall as a 20-story building and has three blades that span 200 feet (61 m) across. The largest wind machines in the world have blades longer than a football field. Wind machines stand tall and wide to capture more wind.

Wind power plants, or wind farms as they are sometimes called, are clusters of wind machines used to produce electricity. A wind farm usually has dozens of wind machines scattered over a large area. Wind farms cannot be built just anywhere, however; their locations must be carefully planned. Wind speed and frequency, local weather conditions, proximity to electrical transmission lines, and local zoning codes must all be taken into consideration.

There are many good sites for wind plants in the United States, including California, Alaska, Hawaii, the Great Plains, and mountainous regions. Scientists at the U.S. Department of Energy say there is enough wind in 37 states to produce electricity. An average wind speed of 14 miles per hour (22.5 km/hr) is needed to convert wind energy into electricity economically. The average wind speed in the United States is 10 miles per hour (16 km/hr).

Because wind speed increases with altitude and over open areas with no windbreaks, good sites for wind farms are the tops of smooth, rounded hills; open plains or shorelines; and mountain gaps that produce wind funneling.

In terms of efficiency, experts have determined that wind machines are just as efficient as most other energy plants, such as coal plants. Wind machines convert 30% to 40% of the wind's kinetic energy into electricity. A coal-fired power plant converts about 30% to 35% of the chemical energy in coal into usable electricity.

Wind power plants are different from power plants that burn fuel, however. Wind plants depend on the availability of wind, as well as the speed of the wind. Therefore, wind machines cannot operate 24 hours a day, 365 days a year. A wind turbine at a typical wind farm operates

Wind is a renewable energy source. These wind turbines are at Tehachapi Pass, California. This wind farm, with 5,000 wind turbines, is the second largest collection of wind generators in the world. The turbines produce enough electricity to meet the needs of 350,000 people every year. *(Courtesy of U.S. Department of Energy)*

65% to 80% of the time, but usually at less than full capacity when the wind speed is not at an optimum level.

Each wind machine can produce enough electricity in a year to provide power for 150 to 400 homes. Currently, wind energy provides about 0.1% of the United State's electricity. That is enough electricity to serve roughly a million households—as many as in a city the size of Houston, Texas. Wind energy is currently the fastest growing energy technology in the world. According to the U.S. Department of Energy, experts expect the production from wind machines to triple in the next few years.

Another positive sign for the wind industry is the growing consumer demand for "green energy." Many utilities around the country now allow customers to voluntarily choose to pay slightly more for electricity generated by renewable sources as an effort to protect the environment. Energy experts believe wind energy will become more in demand in the future.

AIR QUALITY ISSUES

The atmosphere is not only critical to energy development, but even more so to life itself. As the world has progressively become more developed, with rapidly exploding populations, the need for energy to maintain today's lifestyles has impacted one of the Earth's greatest resources. In many parts of the world, air quality has been damaged—this threatens the health of humans and other life-forms. Because development is going to continue, techniques must be developed today in order to protect air quality.

The National Oceanic and Atmospheric Administration (NOAA) operates the Air Resources Laboratory (ARL), which conducts research on processes that relate to air quality and climate. There are many sources of air pollution, such as cars, power plants, factories, small businesses, and household products. Under the **Clean Air Act**, the Environmental Protection Agency (EPA) develops and enforces rules and regulations to minimize pollutants in the atmosphere.

Air pollution affects all living things. It can cause illness, burning eyes and nose, an irritated throat, and breathing problems. Some chemicals in polluted air cause cancer, birth defects, brain and nerve damage, and long-term injury to the lungs and breathing passages. Some air pollutants are so dangerous that accidental releases can cause serious injury or even death.

Air pollution can also damage the environment. Water, plants, and animals have been harmed by air pollution. Air pollutants have also thinned the protective ozone layer above the Earth. This loss of ozone could cause changes in the environment as well as more skin cancer and cataracts (eye damage) in people. Air pollution can damage property and dirty buildings and other structures. Some common pollutants eat away stone and are currently damaging historical and other buildings, monuments, and statues. Air pollution can also cause haze, which reduces visibility in national parks and also sometimes interferes with air traffic.

Most air toxics originate from human-made sources, including mobile sources (cars, trucks, buses), stationary sources (factories, refineries, power plants), and indoor sources (building materials and cleaning solvents). It is for these reasons that the United States adopted the Clean Air Act in 1990.

There are seven common air pollutants: **particulate matter, carbon monoxide**, nitrogen dioxide, sulfur dioxide, lead, volatile organic compounds, and ground-level ozone. Particulate matter—also called particle pollution—is a complex mixture of extremely small particles and liquid droplets. Particle pollution is made up of several components, such as acids (nitrates and sulfates), organic chemicals, metals, and soil or dust particles. The size of the particle is directly linked to its potential for causing health problems. The EPA is concerned about particles that are 10 micrometers in diameter or smaller because those are the particles that generally pass through the throat and nose and enter the lungs. Once inhaled, these particles can affect the heart and lungs and cause serious health effects.

Particulates (dust, smoke, and soot) originate from the burning of wood, diesel, and other fuels; industrial plants; agriculture (plowing, burning off fields); and unpaved roads. Particulates can cause nose and throat irritation, lung damage, bronchitis, and even early death. Particulates are the main source of haze that reduces visibility. The ashes, soot, smoke, and dusts can dirty and discolor structures and other property, including clothes and furniture.

Carbon monoxide (CO) is a colorless, odorless gas that is formed when carbon in fuel is not completely burned. It is a component of motor vehicle exhaust, which contributes about 56% of all CO emissions nationwide. CO concentrations are highest in areas with heavy motor traffic congestion. Other sources include industrial processes (such as metals processing and chemical manufacturing); residential wood burning; and natural sources, such as forest fires. Woodstoves, gas stoves, cigarette smoke, and unvented gas and kerosene space heaters are indoor sources of CO. The highest levels of CO in the outside air typically occur during the colder months of the year when inversion conditions are more frequent. The air pollution becomes trapped near the ground beneath a layer of warmer air.

According to the EPA, CO is a very serious pollutant. When levels in the atmosphere are high, it is poisonous even to healthy people. It can also affect people with heart disease and can affect the central nervous system. When people breathe high levels of CO, they can develop vision problems, reduced ability to work or learn, and reduced manual dexterity. At extremely high levels, CO is poisonous and can cause death. CO also contributes to the formation of smog, which can trigger serious respiratory problems.

Nitrogen oxide (NO_x) is the generic term for a group of highly reactive gases, all of which contain nitrogen and oxygen in varying amounts. Many of the nitrogen oxides are colorless and odorless. One common pollutant, nitrogen dioxide (NO_2), along with other particles in the air can often be seen as a reddish-brown layer (called smog) over many urban areas.

Nitrogen oxides form when fuel is burned at high temperatures, as in a combustion process. The primary man-made sources of NO_x are motor vehicles; electric utilities; and other industrial, commercial, and residential sources that burn fuels. NO_x can also be formed naturally.

NO_x is one of the main ingredients involved in the formation of ground-level ozone. It reacts to form nitrate particles, acid aerosols, as well as carbon dioxide, which also cause respiratory problems. NO_x contributes to the formation of **acid rain**, deteriorates water quality, deteriorates visibility in the atmosphere, reacts to form toxic chemicals, and contributes to global warming. It can be transported over long distances by prevailing winds.

Sulfur dioxide (SO_2) belongs to the family of sulfur oxide gases (SO_x). These gases dissolve easily in water. Sulfur is naturally contained in many materials used in industry, such as oil, coal, lead, iron, zinc, and aluminum. SO_x gases are formed when fuel that contains sulfur, such as coal and oil, is burned, and when gasoline is obtained from oil, or metals are extracted from ore. SO_2 dissolves in water vapor to form acid and interacts with other gases and particles in the atmosphere to form sulfates and other products that can harm humans and the environment.

According to the EPA, more than 65% of SO_2 released to the atmosphere—or more than 13 million tons per year—comes from electric utilities, especially those that burn coal. SO_2 can also come from other industrial sources that commonly use crude oil, coal, or metallic ore. Examples of these types of industries include petroleum refineries, cement manufacturing, and metal-processing facilities. Also, trains, large ships, and some diesel equipment burn high sulfur fuel and release SO_2 emissions to the atmosphere in quantities large enough to be harmful.

SO_2 contributes to respiratory illness and worsens existing heart and lung diseases. It also contributes to the formation of acid rain and adds smog to the atmosphere. Like nitrogen dioxide, it can travel great distances, affecting large areas.

Lead is another pollutant, which has been decreasing since 1978 because of mandated reductions in emissions from cars and trucks. Although the major source of lead used to be from emissions of these vehicles, today, metal-processing plants are generally responsible for most of the lead in the atmosphere.

Lead exposure creates serious cause for concern, especially for young children and infants. It is still found at high levels in some urban and industrial areas today; its deposits in soil and water harm animals and fish. Children and others can be exposed to lead not only through the air, but also through accidentally or intentionally eating soil or paint chips, as well as food or water contaminated with lead. Urban areas with high levels of traffic, trash incinerators, or other industry, as well as areas near lead smelters, battery plants, or industrial facilities that burn fuel, may still have high lead levels in the air.

There are many detrimental health effects caused by lead. For example, it can cause damage to the kidneys, liver, brain and nerves, and other organs. It may lead to osteoporosis (brittle bone disease) and reproductive disorders. Lead can cause seizures, high blood pressure, and anemia (weak blood). If wild or domestic animals ingest lead while grazing, they experience the same kinds of effects as people who are exposed. Because it enters water systems through runoff,

The Clean Air Act

The 1990 Clean Air Act is a piece of U.S. legislation relating to the reduction of smog and atmospheric pollution. It follows the Clean Air Act of 1963, the Clean Air Act Amendment of 1966, the Clean Air Act Extension in 1970, and the Clean Air Act Amendments in 1977.

Although the 1990 Clean Air Act is a federal law covering the entire country, the individual states do much of the work to carry out the act. This law gives individual states the jurisdiction to approve permit applications and fine companies for violating air pollution limits. Under this law, the EPA sets limits on how much of a pollutant can be in the air anywhere in the United States. States are not allowed to have weaker pollution controls than those set for the whole country.

Individual states must develop state implementation plans (SIPs) that explain how they will enforce the Clean Air Act. A state implementation plan is a collection of the regulations a state will use to clean up polluted areas. The states are obligated to notify the public of these plans through hearings and offer the public opportunities to comment on the development of each state implementation plan before it is put into effect. The EPA must approve each SIP, and it also assists the states by providing scientific research, expert studies, engineering designs, and money to support clean air programs.

Air pollution often travels from its source in one state to another state. In many metropolitan areas, people live in one state and work in another, allowing air pollution from cars and trucks to spread throughout the interstate area. The 1990 Clean Air Act provides for interstate commissions on air pollution control. These commissions are to develop regional strategies for cleaning up air pollution.

The act also covers international air pollution issues. The law applies to pollution that originates in Mexico or Canada and drifts into the United States, as well as pollution from the United States that reaches Canada and Mexico.

Source: Environmental Protection Agency

sewage, or industrial waste streams, it can also harm fish and other marine life.

Volatile organic compounds (called VOCs) are another element in smog. Cars are a major source of VOCs. These compounds can cause serious health problems, such as cancer. Scientists at the EPA have determined that they are also harmful to plant life.

Ground-level ozone is the principal component of urban smog. It forms as a chemical reaction of the pollutants NO_x, and VOCs. Unfortunately, it is the cause of breathing problems, reduced lung function, asthma, irritated eyes, stuffy nose, reduced resistance to colds and other infections, and may also speed up the aging of lung tissue. Ground-level ozone also has significant environmental effects; it can harm vegetation and smog can reduce visibility.

Because of these hazards in the atmosphere, the EPA spends a significant amount of time regulating and managing the quality of the atmosphere. One way they accomplish this is through the use of computer modeling. New and existing air pollution sources are modeled for compliance with the National Ambient Air Quality Standards (NAAQS). Mathematical models are developed to predict the dispersion of pollution using computer programming, meteorological input data, and documentation. Air quality models help managers enforce the necessary practices to keep the air clean. Through the use of models, scientists are able to protect the environment from pollutants by providing sound scientific evidence of pollution and potential pollution and create a technical basis for management policies to be put in place to protect this valuable resource.

THE USE AND IMPACT OF WATER AND ATMOSPHERIC RESOURCES

This chapter first looks at the major uses of freshwater and then explores coastal impacts of land use, the threat of overfishing to marine biodiversity, and the harmful effects of oil spills. Next, it focuses on the impacts of severe weather and associated emergency preparedness. Finally, it looks at the greenhouse effect and global climate change issues.

USES OF FRESHWATER

Freshwater is used for consumptive and nonconsumptive purposes. The use of water is considered consumptive if the water is rendered not available for another use. For example, losses to subsurface seepage and evaporation are natural consumptive uses; someone watering their garden in the summer at the hottest part of the day, causing the majority of the water to evaporate is an example of human-caused consumptive use. Dumping oil or other toxins in rivers is also consumptive. When water can be treated and returned as surface water—as is done with sewage—that is generally considered nonconsumptive use, since that water can be put to additional use.

Nearly 70% of worldwide water use is for irrigation. Areas with extremely dry climates depend almost entirely on irrigation water to grow crops and other vegetation. Aquaculture is a small, but growing, agricultural use of water. Aquaculture is the cultivating and harvesting of fish and other marine life. Freshwater commercial fisheries are another agricultural use of water.

As the world population grows, and as demand for food increases, scientists are working on ways to develop more food using less water, such as with improvements in irrigation methods and technologies, better water management, and developing crops that can survive on less water in order to grow.

Roughly 15% of global water use is for industry, such as for power plants (which use water for the cooling of equipment, or for the generation of power directly, such as in hydroelectric facilities). Industries, such as ore and oil refineries, use large amounts of water in chemical processes, and manufacturing plants use water as a solvent.

About 15% of the world's water is used as a household resource. These uses include drinking water, bathing, cooking, sanitation (toilets), and gardening. Most household water is treated and returned to surface water systems, with the exception of water used to grow and maintain landscaping.

Water is used for recreation, such as reservoirs that are used by many people for boating, water skiing, and fishing. Another small, but very important, use of freshwater is for environmental water use, such as the water contained in artificial wetlands, artificial lakes intended to create wildlife habitat, fish ladders around dams, and water releases from reservoirs timed to help fish spawn.

According to the Environmental Protection Agency (EPA), in the United States, the demand for water actually declined in 1985 and has remained fairly steady since then. Changes in technology, in laws, and in the economy, as well as the increased awareness of the need for water conservation, have resulted in the more efficient use of water from America's rivers, lakes, reservoirs, and aquifers.

COASTAL IMPACTS OF LAND USE

As populations continue to grow and land is being developed to accommodate these larger populations, stress is being placed on coastal land and resources. According to experts at the Center for Coastal Environmental Health and Biomolecular Research (an organization within the National Oceanic and Atmospheric Administration, or NOAA), this stress is resulting in depleted fisheries; lost habitat; degraded water quality; and increased loads of chemical, microbial, and organic stressors and sediment runoff. These conditions are found throughout the coastal United States and are some of the most challenging problems coastal resource managers must face today.

Impacts to coastal areas from land use include (1) the introduction of pesticides (toxins used to kill insects) and herbicides (toxins used to kill weeds) to waterways through runoff from people's yards and from agricultural areas; (2) removal of forests, which causes erosion to the bare surface left behind, which, in turn, adds sediment to waterways; (3) the construction of dams, which changes fish habitat and other aquatic ecosystems; and (4) building cities and paving the ground so that water cannot infiltrate in that area. The effects of these impacts vary, but they often affect plant and animal habitat.

Climate change—both natural and human-caused—can affect coastal ecosystems, which weakens the environment's resilience and makes these systems more vulnerable to damage. Altered **sea-level** conditions, water temperature changes, currents, and stratification can lead to changes in salinity, tides, and erosion, which can degrade the system.

Even natural disasters, such as hurricanes, floods, and droughts can destroy coastal communities in an extremely short time period. Strong winds and waves that result from storms alter the freshwater flow and availability, as well as nutrient concentrations, which also impact these areas.

Beach erosion is a serious problem. This erosion was caused by a northeaster on the Outer Banks, North Carolina. *(Photo courtesy of National Oceanic and Atmospheric Agency; photo by Richard B. Mieremet, Senior Advisor, NOAA OSDIA, America's Coastlines Collection)*

According to the EPA, over the past 30 years, the United States has substantially reduced industrial and chemical pollution from point sources; namely, pollution with a clearly identifiable source, such as a discharge pipe or conduit. Tackling the more subtle non-point sources—runoff from major urban areas and agricultural fields—is more difficult because there is not an obvious single location to stop the problem. Potentially harmful chemical pollution and excess nutrient runoff are critical concerns for environmental and land managers in coastal areas.

Coastal erosion is another major problem. Shorelines, beaches, dunes, and barrier islands are often the main defense to protect estuaries, wetlands, bays, and coastal properties against erosional forces (such as hurricanes, storms, and tides). Estuaries, wetlands, coastal swamps, marshlands, and bays are also areas of extensive biological productivity. If erosion damages or destroys these areas, the economy of a region can be hurt. If fisheries are impacted, then a food source for people is taken away. Coastlines can erode many feet in a single year. For example, along the Gulf of Mexico, erosion rates can be as high as 60 feet (18 m) per year, according to the EPA.

Coastal erosion results from the beach interacting with the ocean. A beach does not stay the same from day to day—it is very dynamic. In fact, scientists refer to a beach system as being in *dynamic equilibrium*. This means that sand is moved from one location to another but it does not actually leave the beach areas. For example, winter storms, which generate large waves, may remove significant amounts of sand, creating steep, narrow beaches. In the summer, gentle waves return the sand, widening the beaches and making the slopes more gentle.

The energy in the wave determines the size and the amount of sand that will move and how far it will go. The energy in the wave depends on several factors: (1) on the speed of the wind, (2) how long the wave travels, and (3) if there is anything to block the wave as it moves toward shore. Gentle waves move fine sand, but storm-generated waves can move rocks and boulders. Materials picked up from shoreline areas are deposited wherever the water is slowed down. Because there are so many things that can affect coastal erosion (such as human activity, weather conditions, sea-level rise, and climate change), sand movement changes from year to year.

Coastal erosion creates many problems to coastal communities because valuable property such as businesses and homes can be destroyed by waves if too much sand is removed from the beach. Beach erosion can also destroy the nesting habitat of many threatened or endangered sea turtles and birds.

One way to restore eroded beaches is through a process called beach nourishment. In this process, sand is collected from the ocean bottom several miles from the shore by a dredge—a large floating machine used for scooping up sand and gravel from the ocean floor. The dredge then pipes the sand and gravel to the beach. A mixture of sand and water exits the pipe on the beach, and as water drains away, sand is left behind. Bulldozers move this new sand on the beach until the nourished beach matches the beach before erosion. Over time, this process may have to be repeated.

OVERFISHING—A THREAT TO MARINE BIODIVERSITY

Fishing is important to the livelihood and food security of 200 million people worldwide, especially in developing countries. As many as one in five people on Earth depends on fish as their primary source of protein. According to United Nations (UN) agencies, aquaculture—the farming and stocking of aquatic organisms including fish, mollusks, crustaceans, and aquatic plants—is growing more rapidly than all other animal food producing sectors. Even so, statistics reveal that the main marine fish stocks are threatened globally, because they are being impacted by severe overfishing and environmental degradation.

The magnitude of the problem of overfishing is not always given the attention it deserves. Another downfall is that the rapid growth in demand for fish and fish products is leading to fish prices increasing faster than prices of other meat. This is causing a serious economic impact. Because of the appeal of making a lot of money, large private businesses and governments are operating fisheries, which prevents the small fishing companies and fishing communities all over the world from making an income. In the past ten years, in the North Atlantic region, commercial fish populations of cod, hake, haddock, and flounder have fallen by as much as 95%. Many specialists are recommending zero catches to allow for regeneration of stocks.

According to the United Nations Environment Programme (UNEP) it is estimated that more than 70% of the world's fish species are either fully exploited or depleted. The dramatic increase of destructive fishing techniques worldwide is destroying marine mammals and entire ecosystems. Unfortunately, there are reports that illegal, unreported, and unregulated fishing worldwide are increasing as fishermen try to catch more fish than they are allowed. These problems need to be addressed and plans put into place to ensure sustainable fishing (which means not catching more fish than can be replaced).

OIL SPILLS

According to the U.S. Environmental Protection Agency, every year, millions of gallons of oil are released into the environment, either accidentally or intentionally. This oil comes from tanker accidents, blowouts, or spills at offshore drilling rigs and from runoff and dumping of waste oil by people and industries.

Accidents can occur when transporting oil. When oil gets spilled, it can kill plants and animals and contaminate beaches. Commercial oil spills are especially destructive to the environment. Oil spills into rivers, bays, and the ocean are caused by accidents involving tankers, barges, pipelines, refineries, and storage facilities, usually while the oil is being transported to the users. The EPA recognizes that oil spills can happen for numerous reasons. Spills can be caused by people making mistakes or being careless, equipment breaking down, natural disasters such as hurricanes, deliberate acts by terrorists, countries at war, vandals, or illegal dumpers.

When a spill happens, the oil floats on the surface of the ocean. The oil then spreads out rapidly across the surface into a thin layer called an oil slick. As it continues to spread, the layer thins even more into a sheen, which sometimes looks like a rainbow (similar to sheens in parking lots after a rain).

Oil spills can be very harmful to marine birds and mammals, and can also harm fish and shellfish. Oil destroys the insulating ability of fur-bearing animals, such as sea otters, and the water-repelling abilities of birds' feathers, exposing these animals to harsh environmental elements, such as cold water, cold air, and strong winds. Many birds and mammals also ingest (swallow) oil when they try to clean themselves, which can poison them. Sometimes, thousands of birds and mammals die as a result of oil spills.

Once a spill happens, local, state, and federal government agencies, as well as volunteer organizations, will respond to the incident. The

The *Exxon Valdez* Oil Spill

On March 24, 1989, the *Exxon Valdez* grounded on Bligh Reef, and spilled nearly 11 million gallons (41,639,530 l) of oil into the biologically rich waters of Prince William Sound in Alaska. This was the largest oil spill in the United States. Experts have likened this to the amount of oil it would take to fill more than 9 school gyms, 108 houses, 430 classrooms, or 797 living rooms. More than 33,000 seabirds, nearly 1,000 sea otters, and more than 100 bald eagles were killed.

Even though a major cleanup was enacted, more than 15 years later, oil still persists in certain environments, especially in areas sheltered from weathering processes, such as the subsurface under selected gravel shorelines, and in some soft substrates containing peat.

The *Exxon Valdez* spill served to make the American public aware of environmental health in a new way. The images of heavily oiled shorelines, dead and dying wildlife, and the thousands of workers mobilized to clean beaches reflect what many people felt was the ultimate environmental insult in a previously pristine and biologically rich area. Since the spill, scientists and the public alike have shown concern for the health of the environment and human impacts on fragile ecosystems.

Surface oil today has all but disappeared. However, it is still found in areas beneath the surface and where oil initially penetrated very deeply and was not removed. It is still difficult today for scientists to completely assess the impacts from the disturbance because the ecosystem is so fragile and dynamic. One positive point, however, is that the past 18 years have enabled scientists to learn from misfortune and more fully understand how oil spills should be responded to, how they should be cleaned up, and how to best enable an area to recover.

This is a sea otter—one of the mammals adversely affected by oil spills. When oil saturates their fur, they lose their ability to stay warm in the cold water. The ingestion of oil while trying to clean itself can result in the death of the animal. *(Photo courtesy of National Oceanic and Atmospheric Administration)*

method used for cleanup depends on the specific circumstances of the spill. Road equipment works on sand and beaches, but not in marshes or areas with large boulders. Sometimes, stations are set up where they can clean and rehabilitate wildlife. Sometimes, no response is made because it may cause more harm and damage than help. In the United States, depending on where the spill occurs, either the U.S. Coast Guard or the EPA takes charge of the spill response.

When an oil spill is responded to, several types of countermeasures can be made to reduce the harm of the spill. One method is through the use of *dispersants.* These are chemicals that are applied directly to the spilled oil in order to remove it from the water surface, where oil can be especially harmful. Dispersants work better when the ocean has moderate waves. It is difficult to disperse oil in water that has high waves or that is flat and calm.

Planes flying over the surface of the water drop the dispersant onto the surface. After several weeks, dispersed oil droplets degrade into naturally occurring substances.

SEVERE WEATHER AND EMERGENCY PREPAREDNESS

One aspect of the atmosphere that affects everyone is weather. Different types of severe weather affect different parts of the world at different times of the year. For example, some areas, such as the Great Plains, may experience severe tornadoes. Coastal areas may have to deal with multiple hurricanes and flooding. Certain mountainous areas may be prone to flooding, as well. Islands and coastal areas may have to bear the destructive brunt of **tsunamis**, while other areas may have to contend with extreme heat, and still others severe winter weather.

These extreme events are part of the Earth's dynamic system and atmospheric processes. Because there are many places on Earth that may be affected by one or more of these conditions at any given time, it is important to understand these events and know how to respond and have a plan in place for emergency preparedness.

Tornadoes

Although tornadoes are occasionally reported in other parts of the world, most occur in the United States east of the Rocky Mountains during the spring and summer. However, tornadoes can occur in any state at any time of the year. Nationally, the Department of Health and Human Services (DHS) reports that an average of 800 tornadoes are sighted each year, causing about 80 deaths and more than 1,500 injuries.

A tornado is a violent whirlwind—a rotating funnel of air that extends from a cloud to the ground. Tornadoes can travel for many miles at speeds of 250 miles (402 km) per hour. These storms change direction without warning, randomly destroying homes and power

A tornado strikes near Anadarko, Oklahoma. *(Photo courtesy of National Oceanic and Atmospheric Administration, OAR/ERL/National Severe Storms Laboratory)*

lines, uprooting trees, and even hurling large objects—such as cars or pieces of buildings—over long distances.

Tornadoes usually accompany severe thunderstorms. Occasionally, tornadoes occur during tropical storms or hurricanes. According to the DHS, the path of damage left behind by a tornado averages 9 miles (14 km) long by 200 yards (183 m) wide, but a severe tornado can damage an area up to 50 miles (80 km) long and a mile (1.6 km) wide. The most destructive force in a tornado is the updraft in the funnel. This air is unstable and moves upward at high speeds.

Tornadoes form when unseasonably warm, humid air collides with a cold front, forming intense thunderstorm clouds. As warm air rises within the storm clouds, cooler air rushes in from the sides, creating a

This home in Allison, Texas, was destroyed by a tornado. Tornadoes typically follow erratic paths and may hit one area and miss the adjacent area, only to hit the next area close by when the funnel touches down again. *(Photo courtesy of National Oceanic and Atmospheric Administration Photo Library, NOAA Central Library, OAR/ERL/National Severe Storms Laboratory)*

whirling wind that draws surrounding air toward its center. An area of strong rotation develops 2 to 6 miles (3 to 10 km) wide. Next to appear is a dark, low cloud base called a rotating wall cloud. Moments later, as rotation becomes even stronger, a funnel develops.

Some tornadoes strike rapidly, without time for a tornado warning, and sometimes without a thunderstorm in the vicinity. The following weather signs may mean that a tornado is approaching:

- A dark or green-colored sky
- A large, dark, low-lying cloud

- Large hail
- A loud roar that sounds like a freight train

Tornadoes can be extremely destructive. If a tornado does hit, it is important that people have an emergency preparedness plan already in place. The plan should identify where the best tornado shelters are located and how family members can protect themselves from flying and falling debris.

After a tornado, it is important to shut off the gas and not use matches, lighters, appliances, or light switches until it is confirmed there are no gas leaks. The electricity should also be shut off—sparks from electrical switches could ignite leaking gas and cause an explosion.

Hurricanes

A hurricane—also called a tropical cyclone—is a storm system powered by the heat released when moist air rises and condenses. These storms begin in the tropics and they circulate counterclockwise in the northern hemisphere and clockwise in the southern hemisphere.

Depending on their location and strength, there are various terms by which they are known: *hurricane, typhoon, tropical storm, cyclonic storm,* and *tropical depression.* Hurricanes are capable of producing extremely strong winds, tornadoes, torrential rain, and huge waves that swamp coastal areas, called storm surges. The heavy rains and storm surges create severe floods. Although the effects on human populations can be catastrophic, tropical cyclones have also been known to relieve drought conditions because they transport enormous amounts of moisture. They also carry heat away from the tropics, which is an important mechanism of the global atmospheric circulation that maintains equilibrium in the Earth's troposphere.

When a hurricane hits, people need to already have emergency supplies available. Homes should already be stocked with supplies that may be needed during the emergency period, such as nonperishable food, several large containers of water, and a first-aid kit.

Because it is often necessary to evacuate, people should be prepared for hurricanes. The National Weather Service will issue a hurricane watch when there is a threat to coastal areas of hurricane conditions within 24 to 36 hours of their arrival.

After a hurricane, it is important to protect your health and safety. In order to prevent illness from food, identify and throw away food that may not be safe to eat and store remaining food safely. To prevent illness from water, listen to and follow public announcements and correctly boil or disinfect water when it is called for. It is also wise to be aware of, and be prepared for, carbon monoxide poisoning, floodwater mosquitoes, unstable buildings, and electrical and fire hazards.

Floods

A flood is an overflow of water. There are many causes of flooding. Floods from the sea can cause overflow or overtopping of flood-defenses, such as dikes. Floods from the sea may be caused by a heavy storm (storm surge), high tide, a tsunami, or a combination of the above. As most urban communities are located near the coast, this is a major threat worldwide.

Many rivers that flow over relatively flat land are surrounded by wide floodplains. When heavy rainfall or melting snow causes the river's depth to increase and the river to overflow its banks, large amounts of shallow water can rapidly cover the adjacent floodplain. Rivers prone to flooding have had extensive and elaborate systems of dikes constructed along their shores and surrounding nearby cities. One downfall, however, is that by restraining floodwaters, these dikes can result in much greater flooding downstream and in locations where they break.

Rapidly melting snow and intense periods of rainfall can also cause flash floods. Heavy rain from monsoon rainfall patterns can cause disastrous flooding in some equatorial countries, such as Bangladesh, because of their lengthy periods of rainfall. A flood can also occur when a volcanic eruption melts a large amount of ice and snow quickly. If a snow-capped volcano erupts, the meltwater often picks up substantial amounts of volcanic ash and other debris to become a phenomenon called a *lahar.*

Hurricanes are a source of devastating flooding. With a storm surge, sea flooding as much as 26 feet (8 m) high can be generated by the leading edge of the hurricane when it moves from sea to land. Heavy rainfall also accompanies hurricanes. Because the eye of a hurricane has extremely low pressure, the sea level there can rise a few feet. Floods can also be caused by mammoth waves from tsunamis. Floods are one of the most frequent types of disaster worldwide.

Tsunami

A tsunami is a group of waves that are generated when a body of water (such as an ocean) is rapidly displaced on a massive scale. Several forces can trigger a tsunami. Earthquakes, mass movements above or below water, volcanic eruptions and other underwater explosions, and large meteorite impacts all have this potential. Waves are formed as the displaced water mass moves under the influence of gravity and radiates across the ocean like ripples on a pond. The effects of a tsunami can range from unnoticeable to devastating.

According to the DHS, there are several immediate health concerns, secondary effects, and long-lasting effects associated with tsunamis. The primary public health concerns are clean drinking water, food, shelter, and medical care for injuries. Floodwaters can pose health risks such as contaminated water and food supplies. Loss of shelter leaves people vulnerable to insect exposure, heat, and other environmental hazards. The majority of deaths associated with tsunamis are related to drowning, but traumatic injuries are also a concern. Injuries such as broken arms and legs and head injuries are caused by the physical impact of people being washed into debris such as houses, trees, and other stationary items.

Secondary effects often occurring as a result of tsunamis are outbreaks of infectious diseases. In addition, contaminated water and food supplies, as well as the lack of shelter and medical care, may have a secondary effect of worsening illnesses that already exist in the affected region. Long-term effects are associated with the challenge of restoring normal primary health-care services in many areas, repairing water systems, and providing housing and counseling those people who have experienced trauma from a natural disaster of this magnitude.

Extreme Heat

Temperatures that hover 10 degrees Fahrenheit or more above the average high temperature for the region and last for several weeks are defined as extreme heat. Excessive dry and hot conditions can provoke dust storms and low visibility. Droughts occur when a long period

Tips for Preventing Heat-Related Illness

The best defense is prevention. Effective prevention tips include the following:

- Drink more fluids regardless of your activity level. Do not wait until you are thirsty to drink. Once you are thirsty, that means you have already gone too long without water.

- Do not drink liquids that contain caffeine or large amounts of sugar—these actually cause you to lose more body fluid. Also, avoid very cold drinks, because they can cause stomach cramps.

- Stay indoors, and, if at all possible, stay in an air-conditioned place.

- Electric fans may provide comfort, but when the temperature is 95°F or more (35°C), fans will not prevent heat-related illness. Taking a cool shower or bath, or moving to an air-conditioned place, is a much better way to cool off.

- Wear lightweight, light-colored, loose-fitting clothing.

Source: Centers for Disease Control and Prevention

passes without substantial rainfall. A heat wave combined with a drought can be a very dangerous situation.

Heat-related deaths and illness are preventable, yet annually many people succumb to extreme heat. According to the DHS, from 1979 to 2003, excessive heat exposure caused 8,015 deaths in the United States. In fact, during this time period, more people in the United States died from extreme heat than from hurricanes, lightning, tornadoes, floods, and earthquakes combined.

People suffer heat-related illness when their bodies are unable to compensate and properly cool themselves. The body normally cools itself by sweating. But under some conditions, sweating isn't enough. In such cases, a person's body temperature rises rapidly. This is very serious, because extremely high body temperatures may damage the brain or other vital organs.

Because heat-related deaths are preventable, people need to be aware of who is at greatest risk and what actions can be taken to prevent a heat-related illness or death. The elderly, the very young, and people with mental illness and chronic diseases are at highest risk. However, even young and healthy individuals can succumb to heat if they participate in strenuous physical activities during hot weather. Air-conditioning is the number one protective factor against heat-related illness and death. If a home is not air-conditioned, people can reduce their risk for heat-related illness by spending time in public facilities that are air-conditioned.

Winter Storms

Whenever temperatures drop below normal and wind speed increases, heat can leave the body rapidly. These weather-related conditions can lead to serious health problems. Extreme cold is a dangerous situation that can bring on health emergencies in susceptible people, such as those without shelter or who are stranded, or those who live in a home that is poorly insulated or without heat.

While in your home, it is important to listen to weather forecasts regularly, and check emergency supplies whenever a period of extreme cold is predicted. For fireplaces that are used, the chimney flue needs to be inspected each year. If a fireplace, wood stove, or kerosene heater are going to be used, install a smoke detector and a battery-operated carbon monoxide detector near the area to be heated. Test them monthly, and replace the batteries twice a year.

It is also important to insulate any water lines that run along exterior walls so the water supply will be less likely to freeze. Weatherproof the home by adding weather stripping, insulation, insulated doors and storm windows, or thermal-pane windows. Pet owners should bring pets indoors or provide adequate shelter to keep them warm and make sure that they have access to unfrozen water.

It is also important to conserve heat inside the home by avoiding unnecessary opening of doors or windows. Unused rooms should be closed off and window draperies should be shut at night to help keep the heat in.

Extreme cold can also cause water pipes in the home to freeze and sometimes rupture. When very cold temperatures are expected, all water taps should be left slightly open so they drip continuously (so they will not freeze). When the weather is extremely cold, and especially if there are high winds, people should try to stay indoors. Any necessary trips outside should be as brief as possible.

During extremely cold weather, the DHS has the following recommendations:

- Avoid exertion.
- Understand wind chill and the effects it can have.
- Avoid walking on ice.
- Be safe during recreation by notifying others where you will be if you are going outside for a lengthy period of time.
- Be cautious about travel—do not travel in low-visibility conditions. Use tire chains, and take a mobile phone with you. Always carry additional warm clothing appropriate for the winter conditions.

THE GREENHOUSE EFFECT AND GLOBAL CLIMATE CHANGE

The atmosphere naturally acts as an insulating blanket, which is able to trap enough solar energy to keep the global average temperature within a comfortable range in which to support life. This insulating blanket is a collection of various atmospheric gases.

The framework in which this system works is often called the greenhouse effect because this global system of insulation is similar to that which occurs in a greenhouse nursery for plants. These gases, mainly water vapor (H_2O), carbon dioxide (CO_2), methane (CH_4), and nitrous oxide (N_2O), all act as effective global insulators. These trace gases are relatively transparent to incoming visible light from the sun, yet opaque to the energy radiated from the Earth.

These gases are the reason why the Earth's atmosphere does not scorch during the day and freeze at night. Instead, the Earth's atmosphere contains molecules that absorb the heat and reradiate the heat in all directions, which reduces the heat lost back to space. Greenhouse gas molecules keep the Earth's temperature ranges within comfortable limits. Therefore, without the natural greenhouse effect, life would not be possible on Earth.

Atmospheric scientists began to use the term *greenhouse effect* in the early 1800s as a term used to describe the natural, life-giving phenomenon of the Earth's atmosphere. In fact, it was not until the mid-1950s that the term *greenhouse effect* was used along with the concept of climate change. Today, the term is used in a negative way to refer to the possible impacts of an "enhanced" greenhouse effect—caused by human behavior and actions.

Scientists know that the Earth's climate changes over time. For example, the last ice age ended only about 10,000 years ago. When the Earth entered a warmer climate, agriculture, civilization, industry, and technology enabled the standard of living to evolve as we know it today.

Although climate naturally varies over time, scientists are more concerned today because they believe the natural greenhouse effect is being enhanced by human activities—especially the burning of fossil fuels and the subsequent addition of CO_2 to the air. Since the 1800s, societies have been burning huge amounts of fossil fuels to power developing industrial and technological sectors. As a result, because CO_2 is a powerful greenhouse gas, it makes the atmosphere's temperature steadily rise. In fact, climatologists around the world have detected a steady, but currently small, increase in global average temperatures for the past few decades; and according to the EPA, six of the last ten years were the hottest on record.

A major danger to this is that if the temperature rises, the entire global climate system powered by heat energy will also change. Most atmospheric scientists believe that the global climate is warming at least partially because of a build-up of CO_2 from fossil fuel use. Many scientists and other environmentalists are working on ways of lowering the CO_2 levels being added to the atmosphere by promoting the use of alternative, renewable energy such as solar and wind energy. They believe that controlling CO_2 levels is critical in order to sustain fragile ecosystems and life on Earth.

THE IMPORTANCE OF WATER AND ATMOSPHERIC RESOURCES

There are many goods and services provided by the oceans, other water bodies, and the atmosphere. Many of them have already been discussed, such as food, freshwater, drinking water, clean air, salt, minerals, transportation, recyclable power, and petroleum, to name a few. This chapter will discuss additional goods and services. It will look at the importance of wetlands and explore the incredible beauty and vitality of coral reefs. It will then focus on tourism, recreation, and aesthetic values. Finally, it will focus on the roles of education, research, and employment in regard to these resources.

COASTAL AND FRESHWATER WETLANDS

Wetland is a term used to describe marshes, swamps, bogs, and other wet areas. Wetlands are found in flat vegetated areas; in depressions on the landscape; and between water and dry land along the edges of streams, rivers, lakes, and coastlines.

The Importance of Coastal Wetlands

Important function	Application
Water quality	Some wetlands contribute to improving water quality by removing excess nutrients and many chemical contaminants. These improvements occur due to uptake by the plants and binding with soil particles.
Barriers to waves and erosion	Coastal wetlands reduce the impact of storm tides and waves before they reach upland areas.
Flood storage	Coastal wetlands can store floodwater and release it slowly, lowering flood peaks.
Sediment control	Reduced flood flow provided by coastal wetlands allows floodwater to deposit sediment, instead of transporting sediment into waterways where it can pose a water quality problem.
Wildlife habitat	Coastal wetlands can support wide varieties of wildlife.
Fish and shellfish	Coastal wetlands are important spawning and nursery areas for fish and shellfish, and provide sources for commercial fishing.
Sanctuary for rare and endangered species	Protection of wetlands often means providing survival habitats for endangered animals. Nearly half of the threatened and endangered species in the United States rely on wetlands for their survival.
Aesthetic value	The natural beauty of wetlands is a source of visual enjoyment and can be appreciated through observation, art, and poetry.
Education and research	The rich ecosystems of wetlands are natural locations for biological research and observation.
Recreation	Wetlands provide sites for hunting, fishing, canoeing, and observing wildlife.
Food production	Wetlands have potential for the production of plant products, including marsh vegetation, and for aquaculture. Wetlands also produce great volumes of food in the form of decaying plant and animal matter or detritus.
Water supply	With the growth of urban areas, wetlands are becoming more valuable as sources for water.

Source: U.S. Environmental Protection Agency

Wetlands encompass a wide variety of aquatic habitats. Swamps, marshes, bogs, prairie potholes, and floodplains are all names for ecosystems known as wetlands. Wetlands are the places where land and

The Importance of Freshwater Wetlands

Important function	Application
Water quality	Some wetlands contribute to improving water quality by removing excess nutrients and many chemical contaminants.
Flood conveyance	Wetlands can form natural floodways that allow floodwater to move downstream without causing damage.
Flood storage	Freshwater wetlands can store floodwater and release it slowly, lowering flood peaks.
Wildlife habitat	Inland wetlands can support wide varieties of wildlife.
Sanctuary for rare and endangered species	Protection of wetlands often means providing survival habitats for endangered animals. Nearly half of the threatened and endangered species in the United States rely on wetlands for their survival.
Aesthetic value	The natural beauty of wetlands is a source of visual enjoyment.
Recreation	Wetlands provide sites for fishing, canoeing, and observing wildlife.
Education and research	The ecosystems of wetlands are natural locations for biological research and observation.
Water supply	With the growth of urban areas, wetlands are becoming more valuable as sources for water supply.
Food production	Wetlands have potential for the production of marsh vegetation and aquaculture.
Timber production	Properly managed, wetlands can provide good sources of timber.
Historical value	Some wetlands were locations for Native American settlements and provide great historical and archaeological value.

Source: U.S. Environmental Protection Agency

water meet; they provide homes to some of the richest biodiversity on Earth. They are found all over the world, from the humid tropics to the frozen plains.

Wetlands provide a very important service. They prevent flooding by holding water, similar to a sponge. Because of this, wetlands are able to keep river levels normal and filter and purify the surface water. Wetlands hold excess water during storms and whenever water levels are high. When water levels are low, wetlands are able to slowly release water. They may be temporarily flooded each day—as with tidal marshes—or be filled seasonally with water from melting snow.

In the past, wetlands were generally considered to be wastelands—often referred to as swamps. In fact, as the United States was settled and people moved west, swamps and marshes were considered unproductive nuisances. Many were drained in order to be replaced by farmland, railroads, and roads. In recent decades, however, people have come to realize their value.

Wetlands are also crucial to wildlife habitat. They serve as important migratory rest stops. Many migratory birds stop at wetlands on the way to their winter and summer nesting grounds. Thousands of birds use them during the spring and fall.

CORAL REEFS

Coral reefs are created by tiny marine animals called polyps, which are relatives of jellyfish and sea anemones. They live in warm, shallow waters and create brilliantly colored structures called coral reefs. Polyps are soft creatures with hard outer cases of calcium carbonate called coral. This hard layer serves as protection for the polyps. When they die, they leave the coral behind. The calcium carbonate remains become a permanent deposit. For this reason, the coral reefs enlarge and can become a very complex structure. Over time, millions of corals build up to form large walls called reefs. The coral polyps form various kinds of reef structures that have been given names like "star," "elk horn," or "brain" coral. A nonreef building coral, *octocoral*, can look like trees and shrubs, forming "sea fans" and "sea whips."

Coral reefs are unique and extremely biodiverse habitats. Popular areas for scuba diving, many reefs are currently in jeopardy from overuse, pollution, and global warming. *(Photo courtesy of National Oceanic and Atmospheric Administration, Florida Keys National Marine Sanctuary, Coral Kingdom Collection)*

Coral reefs are among the most biologically rich ecosystems on Earth. So far, scientists have described about 4,000 species of fish and 800 species of reef-building corals that live in them. Experts, however, believe they have just begun to catalog the total number of species actually found within these habitats.

Coral reefs are one of the wonders of nature because of their enchanting beauty and unusual biology. Many scientists consider them to be second only to tropical rain forests as incubators and protectors of biodiversity.

Coral reefs have been around for about 200 million years, and have survived eons of storm-induced damage and sea animal predation. Unfortunately, their survival today is becoming less certain. The Global Coral Reef Monitoring Network says that about 25% of coral reefs worldwide have been effectively lost, and another 40% could potentially be lost by 2010 unless urgent action is taken.

Warming oceans, pollution from human activities, damage from careless tourists and fishermen—even increased ultraviolet radiation from the sun due to the depletion of ozone in the upper atmosphere—have been blamed for extensive illness and death in the coral population. Corals are especially vulnerable because they are near coastlines and near the surface of the ocean. There are fewer healthy coral colonies on the planet than even a few decades ago, according to marine scientists. One of the most frequently studied causes of coral death is known as *coral bleaching*. When stressed by overly warm water, coral polyps lose their pigment and expose the white calcium carbonate structure underneath. When this process continues long enough, the reefs become sick or die.

Corals also have natural predators and diseases. But while these and human damage from recreation or fishing are major threats to coral, most observers agree that an altered environment plays an important role. In addition to stresses due to changes in ocean temperature, reefs are increasingly exposed to sewage, agricultural runoff, and associated algae blooms near coastal shorelines. All of these inputs have a detrimental effect on corals.

Sediment that clouds the water is also bad for coral, and increasing amounts are flowing into the ocean because of erosion on land caused by human behavior. Unsustainable and damaging fishing practices, including drag netting, trawling, and the use of cyanide and explosives to kill fish, are also destroying reefs.

Reefs do not grow quickly—they typically grow from 1 to 16 feet (0.3 to 4.9 m) every thousand years. Healthy coral reefs promote species diversity. Funguses, sponges, mollusks, oysters, clams, crabs, shrimps, sea urchins, turtles, and many fish seek food and shelter amid reefs. The architecture of corals provides reef fish protection from carnivorous species, such as sharks and barracudas. Sea cucumbers, worms, and mollusks burrow into the reef-generated sand to hide from their enemies. According to Worldwatch Institute, reefs include only 0.3% of the ocean area, but one out of every four ocean species thus far identified is a reef dweller, including at least 65% of marine fish species.

Attempts to restore coral reefs and to better manage their biological richness include efforts to inventory and protect the structures themselves. Changes in human activity also play an important role. Watershed management practices, including protection and conservation of wetlands with their mud flats, mangrove forests, and sea grasses, can help the estuarine system, including corals, to remain clean and healthy.

Coral reefs have come to the attention of the public only recently. Governments and private-sector organizations have taken note of the deterioration of the world's reefs and are trying to find solutions. In 1994, the U.S. government helped found the International Coral Reef Initiative—a partnership designed to address threats to coral reefs. In 1996, the U.S. Coral Reef Initiative was launched to support these efforts, and in 1998, the president issued an executive order directing U.S. government agencies to protect coral reefs. This has resulted in several actions designed to protect this valuable resource and the unique services it provides. Reefs are being inventoried and mapped, and scientific research, restoration, and working with other countries have all come about because of these initiatives.

TOURISM, RECREATION, AND AESTHETIC VALUES

Tourism is one of the fastest growing businesses in the world. Coastal areas have experienced a dramatic increase in activity as vacationers visit exotic beaches and other coastal areas to boat, scuba dive, collect sea shells, or just relax on the beach under a palm tree. In these instances, the tourism industry is based largely on natural resources. If tourism is not managed in an environmentally sound way, then the ecosystem can be damaged. If tourism is managed sustainably (where it does not harm the environment), it can actually promote conservation of the environment, as more people become environmentally aware and make a conscious decision to behave in an environmentally friendly way (such as not dumping garbage on the beaches or in the ocean, not harming fragile habitats, and not damaging coral reefs while scuba diving). Ecotourism and cultural tourism are a new trend

A sport gaining in popularity is powered parachute flying. The ultralight aircraft can soar thousands of feet above the ground, while moving at about 30 miles an hour (48km/hr). *(Photo courtesy of Nature's Images)*

Fishing is a popular activity at many lakes, such as this one in the Wasatch National Forest, Utah. *(Photo courtesy of Nature's Images)*

Tourists can explore the ocean depths from a touring submarine, such as this one off the coast of Honolulu, Hawaii. Submarines make it possible for people to see coral reefs and a multitude of marine life, such as sharks, up close. *(Photo courtesy of Nature's Images)*

wound, they become a soft gel and make a warm, moist environment for natural healing.

- Calcitonon for treating bone disorders was modeled after a protein from coho salmon. This hormone, also secreted by humans but in a much less potent form, slows bone breakdown.

- Tetrodotoxin for neuroscience research is collected from puffer fish and other marine organisms. It is a useful tool because it is a very potent nerve inhibitor.

- Adhesive for immobilizing cells and tissues for research is made from mussels' byssal fibers—the anchors that mussels secrete to fasten themselves to rocks. The byssal-fiber "glue" has many biotechnological uses.

- Drug purity tests can be done simply with an extract of horseshoe crab blood cells, which indicates the presence of dangerous bacterial toxins.

- Absorbable sutures contain chitosan, made from shells of shrimps and crabs. In addition to sutures that speed healing after surgery, chitosan has dozens of uses in food, cosmetics, drugs, farm products, and water treatment.

- ARA-C, an antileukemia drug, was modeled on compounds taken from Caribbean sponges. It was one of the first drugs marketed in the United States that had an ocean connection.

- Bone substitute for speeding regrowth of bone grafts is available from corals. Coral skeletal structure is remarkably similar to human bone.

EDUCATION, RESEARCH, AND EMPLOYMENT

Three other important services provided by water and atmospheric resources are education, research, and employment. These three services touch people's lives every day in some form or another—whether it is research modeling climate, discovering ecosystems and learning about their importance, creating useful products, or promoting environmental awareness for a better tomorrow.

One of the most successful educational programs ever launched was the Sea World Parks, such as the one in San Diego, California. Since its beginning in 1964, Sea World has grown from a small collection of marine animals into one of the largest and most respected marine zoological collections in the world.

Through the interaction between the marine animals, trainers, and public visitors, there are numerous displays of the beauty of the oceans and the life contained within them. Sea World is heavily involved in public education and in several environmental partnerships for the conservation of marine resources. Some of their partners include the National Geographic Society, the National Fish and Wildlife Foundation, the National Wildlife Federation, the Nature Conservancy, the American Bird Conservancy, Bat Conservation International, Cheetah Conservation Fund, Ducks Unlimited, Earthwatch Institute, and the Smithsonian National Zoological Park.

Sea World also operates a premier research facility—the Hubbs-Sea World Research Institute. It is dedicated to ensuring that future generations experience the benefits of a healthy environment by conserving the ecological integrity of the world's oceans and estuaries—a concept called stewardship. By protecting these environments, the Institute builds a solid foundation for marine-based economies, sustainable fisheries, public recreation, transportation, tourism, and quality of life.

The Institute conducts research in four principal areas: ecology, physiology, bioacoustics, and aquaculture. Through the study of ecology, it is possible to gain an understanding of how animals inhabit the oceans, so that human impacts can be minimized. They believe that conserving biological diversity, assessing animal health, and long-term ecosystem studies are all important components to understanding and protecting the marine environment for future generations.

The study of physiology enables researchers to understand ocean migratory patterns, foraging behavior, and critical habitat in order to

The Sea World Shamu show has thrilled audiences for decades. Trainers, such as the one in this photo, spend hundreds of hours with the orcas, developing a bond that enables this trainer to stand on Shamu's nose while it lifts him out of the water. *(Photo courtesy of Nature's Images)*

sustain biological diversity of the ocean. Scientists in the field of bio-acoustics are working to understand how noise affects animals and how these effects can be lessened. Their study of aquaculture is focused on sustainable fisheries management and stock replenishment.

Sea World also offers hands-on experiences for their guests, as shown here at the sea star pond. The park provides many opportunities for learning about marine life, ocean ecology, and conservation of natural resources. *(Photo courtesy of Nature's Images)*

The Hubbs-Sea World Research Institute also offers educational information to the public and has immensely helped people understand the concepts of sustainable ecosystems, complex interactions between systems, and why certain marine species are threatened, endangered, and extinct, as well as solutions to these problems.

Sea World also manages a search and rescue operation. They have been extensively involved in marine animal rescues (such as the manatee), and have rehabilitated many sick, injured, and stranded animals in the wild, such as dolphins, whales, penguins, and sea turtles.

Marine scientists conduct research of these resources for a number of reasons. One major area of research is in understanding the effects the atmosphere and oceans have on climate change. In order to do this, they conduct research on the ocean systems to understand how the ocean transports heat, supplies energy to the atmosphere, causes chemical reactions, supports a diversity of life, and what kind of role it plays in stabilizing global environments.

Marine scientists also study atmospheric systems, such as the complexities of the circulation of heat in the atmosphere, as well as substances (such as water and carbon dioxide). Scientists still need more data on the portion of the atmosphere above the ocean, so that they can better understand the meteorological phenomena that exist there.

Ocean circulation is another area of important research, such as studying the effects of El Niño, global ocean circulation, and the influence of the oceans on climate. This research makes use of sophisticated computer models.

From an ecological standpoint, research is currently being conducted on water quality, physical oceanography, the health of fisheries worldwide, and issues concerning sediment transport due to hurricanes, shoreline stability, and distribution of sand resources.

Many scientists believe the following are the most critical areas needing attention and research concerning the world's oceans:

- Overfishing
- Ocean warming and rising sea levels
- Marine pollution
- Eutrophication (depletion of oxygen levels which kill ocean life)
- Coral reefs
- Ocean noise (low-frequency active sonar can harm some species of whales)
- Carbon dioxide (rising acid levels harm fragile sea life, such as corals)
- Protected areas (designating additional areas for protection)

- Marine biodiversity and extinction prevention
- Invasive species control and habitat protection

Scientists have many concerns about the future of these resources and the results of overuse. For example, with fish stocks being depleted by overfishing, fishing becomes more difficult. This, in turn, leads to people using poisons and explosives, which then lead to the destruction of species and their ecosystems. Concerning ocean warming, the top half-mile (0.8 km) of the ocean has warmed dramatically in the past 40 years as a result of rising greenhouse gases. Scientists believe global warming is the single greatest threat to corals and other sea life. They believe that 20% of the world's reefs are not likely to recover and another 50% are in jeopardy. Through continued research, it is possible to study and set aside protected areas through the establishment of marine sanctuaries.

Scientists also conduct research on the atmosphere. Computer modeling is used to study the effects of pollution, atmospheric circulation, and the effects of climate. Other atmospheric scientists interested in physics conduct research on the geomagnetic field, magnetosphere, ionizing radiation and energy levels, and the effects of solar radiation on life on Earth.

One unique phenomena of the atmosphere that is of interest to scientists is that of the aurora borealis (northern lights) and aurora australis (southern lights). An *aurora* is the collective name given to the photons (light) emitted by atoms, molecules, and ions that have been excited by energetically charged particles (principally electrons) traveling along magnetic field lines into the Earth's upper atmosphere. Auroras result from the interaction of the solar wind with the Earth's magnetic field.

The amazing color displays and formations are produced by the solar wind—a stream of electrons and protons coming from the sun—as it collides with gases in the upper atmosphere. These collisions produce electrical discharges, which energize atoms of oxygen and nitrogen, causing the release of different colors of light. The Earth's magnetic

This beautiful display of light is an aurora australis appearing over South Pole Station, Antarctica. *(Photo courtesy of National Oceanic and Atmospheric Administration; photo by Commander John Bortniak, NOAA Corps Collection)*

field channels these charges toward the poles. Variations in sunspot activity can enhance the auroral discharge adding to the intensity of the displays. Through the study of these phenomena, scientists are able to learn more about electromagnetic radiation, radio waves, solar flares, the composition of the atmosphere, and worldwide communication.

MANAGEMENT OF WATER AND ATMOSPHERIC RESOURCES

In order to maintain the quality of atmospheric and water resources, they must be managed in a responsible way. Without proper planning, management, and enforcement of quality standards, these resources could well be rendered unusable. This chapter looks at management issues concerning these resources. It begins by looking at water resources management, water quality standards, watershed management, waste and storage management, coastal and fisheries management, and the special designation and role of wild and scenic rivers. Then it examines management issues concerning the atmosphere, such as pollution control, mobile sources of human-caused air pollution, thermal pollution and the heat island effect, acid rain, and indoor air pollution.

WATER QUALITY MANAGEMENT

Different quality standards may be applied to water, depending on how it is used. For example, water can be of high enough quality for livestock to drink but not be pure enough for humans to consume. Or, water may provide a healthy environment for bass, bluegill, and other lake fish while not being cold enough or having enough oxygen content to support trout.

Laws involving water quality date back as far as 1914. The first federal law dealing exclusively with water quality was passed in 1948. During the 1960s, amendments provided for federal water quality standards and for increased funding for research. As water pollution increased, three very important environmental laws were passed.

The National Environmental Policy Act of 1969 (NEPA) required federal agencies to consider the environmental impacts of their actions. All federal agencies must prepare environmental impact statements to assess the impacts of major federal actions, such as large building or industrial projects.

The federal Water Pollution Control Act (Clean Water Act), which was passed in 1972, and was amended in 1977, 1981, and 1987, provides the basis for water quality standards today. The Clean Water Act (CWA) also established the National Pollutant Discharge Elimination System (NPDES). The Safe Drinking Water Act (SDWA), passed in

The Safe Drinking Water Act

The Safe Drinking Water Act (SDWA) is a U.S. federal law passed by the Congress on December 16, 1974. It is the main federal law that ensures safe drinking water for Americans. With this act, the Environmental Protection Agency (EPA) is allowed to set the standards for drinking-water quality and oversees all of the states, localities, and water suppliers who implement these standards.

SDWA applies to every public water system in the United States. There are currently more than 160,000 public water systems providing water to almost all Americans at some time in their lives. The SDWA requires the EPA to establish National Primary Drinking Water Regulations (NPDWRs) for contaminants that may cause adverse public health effects.

1974, requires public drinking-water systems to protect drinking-water sources, provide water treatment, monitor drinking water to ensure proper quality, and notify the public of contamination problems. This act serves to establish drinking-water standards.

Water resource management is important in order to manage and integrate a wide variety of uses for water, such as hydropower, drinking water, sanitation, irrigation, and industrial uses. Proper management ensures an adequate clean water supply is available.

One of the most important uses of water, where high quality is critical, is as drinking water. Although drinking water varies from place to place, the United States has one of the safest water supplies in the world. There is no such thing as pure water. In nature, all water contains some impurities. As water flows in streams, sits in lakes, and filters through layers of soil and rock in the ground, it dissolves or absorbs the substances that it touches. Some substances are harmless, such as those in the "mineral water" that many people enjoy drinking. At certain levels, however, minerals are considered contaminants. Because of this, water quality must not only be well-managed, but monitored on a regular basis.

In cities, drinking water comes from surface water sources, such as lakes, rivers, and reservoirs. In rural areas, many people get their drinking water pumped from a well. When managing drinking water, it is important to manage the entire watershed, because the entire drainage can have an effect on water quality. A watershed includes the water and all the surrounding ground from which the water drains. For example, if a stream empties into a river that is used for drinking water, the entire stream's quality, even though far away, must be managed.

Water quality is critically impacted from everything that goes on within the watershed. Mining, forestry, agriculture, grazing, ranching, construction, urban runoff from streets, parking lots, chemically treated lawns and gardens, failing septic systems, and improperly treated municipal sewage discharge all affect water quality. Reducing pollution and protecting water quality requires identifying, regulating, monitoring, and controlling potential pollutants. Examples of good management practices in these types of situations include protecting stream banks and shorelines by maintaining vegetated buffer strips, which filter contaminants and reduce erosion; treating all wastes to remove harmful pollutants; or using grass-lined catchment basins in urban areas to trap sediment and pollutants.

When a water supplier takes untreated water from a river or reservoir, the water often contains dirt and tiny pieces of leaves and other organic matter, as well as trace amounts of certain contaminants. When the water reaches a treatment plant, water suppliers often add chemicals called coagulants to the water. These chemicals cause dirt and other contaminants to form clumps and settle to the bottom. The water then flows through a filter for removal of the smallest contaminants, such as viruses and giardia (a flagellate protozoan inhabiting the intestines of various mammals).

The most common drinking-water treatment, considered by many to be the most important scientific advancement of the twentieth century, is disinfection. Most water suppliers add chlorine or another disinfectant to kill bacteria and other germs. Because management of safe drinking water is so important, the Safe Drinking Water Act gives the U.S. Environmental Protection Agency (EPA) the responsibility for setting national drinking-water standards that protect the health of the 250 million people who get their water from public water systems.

Bottled water is the fastest growing drink choice in the United States, and Americans spend billions of dollars each year to buy it. The taste and quality of both bottled water and tap water depend on the source and quality of the water, including its natural mineral content and how, or if, the water is treated.

Even bottled water must meet specific Food and Drug Administration (FDA) standards. For instance, bottled water must meet FDA standards for physical, chemical, microbial, and radiological contaminants. When the EPA sets a new standard for a contaminant in tap water, the FDA must establish a new standard for the same contaminant in bottled water or find that the EPA's new standard is not applicable to bottled water.

Drinking-water utilities today find themselves facing new responsibilities due to concerns over water system security and counter-terrorism. The EPA is committed to the safety of public drinking-water supplies and has taken numerous steps to work with utilities, other government agencies, and law enforcement to minimize threats.

The Public Health Security and Bioterrorism Preparedness and Response Act of 2002 requires that all community water systems serving more than 3,300 people evaluate their susceptibility to potential threats and identify corrective actions. The EPA has provided assistance to help utilities with these so-called Vulnerability Assessments.

Wastewater management is another important component of water management. Wastewater is not just sewage—it is all the water used in the home that ends up going down the drain and out of the house into the local sewage system. This includes water to wash your face and hands, water to brush your teeth, water from the bathtub and shower, water you let run from the tap while you wait for it to get cold enough to drink, water from the toilets, water from the dishwasher, and water from the clothes washer. Individually, all these uses may seem minor, but in reality, they all add up—and this water must be properly treated as wastewater before it can be used again.

At wastewater treatment plants, this water is treated before it is allowed to be returned to the environment, lakes, or streams. Most treatment plants have primary treatment (physical removal of visible solids) and secondary treatment (the biological removal of dissolved solids).

After primary and secondary treatment, municipal wastewater is usually disinfected using chlorine (or other disinfecting compounds, or occasionally ozone or ultraviolet light). An increasing number of wastewater facilities also employ tertiary (third phase) treatment, often using advanced treatment methods. Tertiary treatment may include processes to remove nutrients such as nitrogen and phosphorus, and carbon adsorption to remove chemicals.

Certain land use practices can minimize negative impacts to the environment. For example, planting trees and other vegetation to protect soil and reduce erosion; fencing livestock to prevent access to streams; properly treating animal wastes; minimizing use of fertilizers and pesticides; properly treating all waste products from industries; using less harmful chemicals and other products in homes, businesses, and industries; and reducing, reusing, and recycling commercial products can all help reduce water pollution.

COASTAL MANAGEMENT

Coastal areas include oceans and coasts, bays and estuaries, and lakes. They are economically, politically, and socially critical places. More than half of the U.S. population lives near the coasts. Coastal areas are the hubs of commerce and major transportation networks worldwide. The coasts are used by millions of Americans each year for recreation and to support tourist trade.

Coastal areas must also be carefully monitored. Plans must be put in place that balance competing demands for recreation, tourism, development, commercial growth, environmental protection, transportation, and fisheries.

Offshore energy resources must also be carefully managed so that coastal wetlands will not be damaged. Other aspects that must be managed include physical disruption to bottom-dwelling marine communities, discharge of contaminants and toxic pollutants present in drilling muds, emissions of pollutants from fixed facilities, seismic exploration and noise impacts on marine life, and the ecological effects of large oil spills.

WILD AND SCENIC RIVERS

In the 1960s, people began to become aware that our nation's rivers were being dammed, dredged, diverted, and polluted at an alarming rate. In 1968, Congress passed the Wild and Scenic Rivers Act, declaring it to be the policy of the United States that "*certain selected rivers of the Nation which, with their immediate environments, possess outstandingly remarkable scenic, recreational, geologic, fish and wildlife, historic, cultural or other similar values, shall be preserved in free-flowing condition, and that they and their immediate environments shall be protected for the benefit and enjoyment of present and future generations.*"

Many thrill seekers, such as these rafters traveling down the Colorado River in eastern Utah, enjoy white-water rafting on the nation's most scenic and beautiful rivers. *(Photo courtesy of Bureau of Land Management, photo by Kelly Rigby)*

The act established three distinct classes of river areas: (1) wild river areas, which are unpolluted areas that do not have dams built across them and are only accessible by trail; (2) scenic river areas, which are undeveloped areas not blocked by dams but that can be reached by road; and (3) recreational river areas, which may have a dam across them and can be easily accessed by road or railroad. Their shorelines may also have developed areas along them.

The Wild and Scenic Rivers Act has helped to protect some of this country's premiere rivers. Though each river designation is different and each management plan is unique, the idea behind the Wild and Scenic River Act is not to lock up a river like a wilderness designation and halt its use and development, but rather to preserve the character of a river. Based on this requirement, any recreational use must be compatible with preservation goals.

The Wild and Scenic Rivers System is managed by an Interagency Coordinating Council, which is composed of representatives of the four wild and scenic rivers administering agencies—the Bureau of Land Management, the National Park Service, the U.S. Fish and Wildlife Service, and the USDA Forest Service. Today, there are 164 designated rivers, with 11,302 total miles (18,186 km). Of this, 5,350 miles (8,610 km) are designated wild; 2,457 miles (3,954 km) are designated scenic; and 3,495 miles (5,624 km) are designated as recreational.

AIR POLLUTION CONTROL

The air we breathe can be contaminated with pollutants from many factories, vehicles, and power plants, to name a few sources. Scientists and health professionals are extremely concerned about these pollutants because of the harmful effects they can have on people's health and the health of the environment. Their impact depends on many factors, including how much air pollution people are exposed to, how long they are exposed, and how strong the pollutants are. The effects of air pollutants can be minor and reversible (such as eye irritation) or debilitating (such as aggravation of asthma) and even fatal (such as cancer).

Since 1970, the Clean Air Act has provided the necessary guidelines for protecting people and the environment from the harmful effects of air pollution. A key component of the Clean Air Act is a requirement that the EPA significantly reduce daily, "routine" emissions of the most potent air pollutants that are known or suspected to cause serious health problems such as cancer or birth defects. Air pollutants are commonly called air toxics.

Scientists at the EPA estimate that millions of tons of toxic pollutants are released into the air each year. Unfortunately, most of these pollutants come from man-made sources, including both mobile sources (cars, buses, trucks) and stationary sources (factories, refineries, power plants). There are some pollutants, however, that are released to the atmosphere because of natural processes, such as forest fires. According to the EPA, emissions from stationary sources constitute almost one half of all man-made air toxics emissions.

"Major" sources are defined as sources that emit 10 tons per year of any of the listed toxic air pollutants. These sources include chemical plants, steel mills, oil refineries, and hazardous waste incinerators. These sources may release air toxics from equipment leaks, when materials are transferred from one location to another or during discharge through emissions stacks or vents. The most vulnerable place to be in relation to these sources is downwind, because the pollutants released into the atmosphere drift downwind, contaminating the areas they flow over.

"Area" sources consist of smaller sources, each releasing smaller amounts of toxic pollutants into the air. These include places like local dry cleaners and gas stations. Although each source may not be big, the combined total of many sources all releasing pollutants can add up and quickly become a serious problem.

Besides wind, other factors come into play once a toxic pollutant is released to the atmosphere. For example, the weather, the terrain, and the chemical and physical properties of a pollutant determine how far it is transported; its concentration at various distances from the source; what kind of physical and chemical changes it experiences; and whether it will degrade, remain airborne, or deposit on land or water.

People are exposed to toxic air pollutants in many ways that can pose health risks. The following list shows some of the ways harmful exposure can occur:

- Breathing contaminated air.
- Eating contaminated food products, such as fish from contaminated waters; meat, milk, or eggs from animals that fed on contaminated plants; and fruits and vegetables grown in contaminated soil on which air toxics have been deposited.
- Drinking water contaminated by toxic air pollutants.
- Eating contaminated soil. (Young children are especially vulnerable).
- Touching contaminated soil, dust, or water.

Once toxic air pollutants enter the body, some of the more persistent types accumulate in body tissues. Depending on which air toxics an individual is exposed to, health effects can vary widely. The effects can include damage to the immune system, as well as neurological, reproductive, developmental, and respiratory problems.

In 1990, amendments to the Clean Air Act mandated a more practical approach to reducing emissions of toxic air pollutants. Instead of using a chemical-by-chemical approach to treating toxics, the EPA developed regulations that require pollution sources to meet specific emissions limits that are based on emissions levels already being achieved by many similar sources in the country. For existing sources of pollutants, their standards must equal the average emissions limitations currently achieved by the best performing 12% of sources in that source category.

For new sources of pollutants, their standards must equal to the level of emissions control that is currently achieved by the best-controlled similar source. As technology improves, and it becomes possible to lower the amount of toxics through the use of new methods, pollutant sources must meet those stricter guidelines if the EPA resets the tolerable pollutant limits.

Some of the air toxics regulations have the added benefit of reducing ground-level ozone (urban smog) and particulate matter. Reductions of smog-causing pollutants and particulate matter are important because of the health and environmental problems they can cause, such as respiratory problems, lung damage, increased infection, and premature death. In addition, many of these pollutants can contribute significantly to impaired visibility in places such as national parks that are valued for their scenic views and recreational opportunities.

MOBILE SOURCES OF AIR POLLUTION

A significant source of air pollution that adds CO_2 to the Earth's troposphere is from mobile sources. *Mobile sources* is a term used to describe vehicles, engines, and equipment that generate air pollution and that move, or can be moved, from one place to another. On-road, or highway, sources include vehicles used on roads for transportation of passengers or freight. On-road vehicles may use gasoline, diesel fuel, or alternative fuels, such as alcohol or natural gas; off-road equipment and vehicles can be fueled with diesel fuel, gasoline, propane, or natural gas.

In the United States, there are many sources of air pollution, such as engines, industries, and commercial operations. Pollutants enter the atmosphere through combustion and fuel evaporation. These sources are the primary cause of air pollution in urbanized areas. Mobile sources contribute many different types of hazardous air pollutants, such as carbon monoxide, hydrocarbons, nitrogen oxides, particulate matter, air toxics, and greenhouse gases. According to the EPA, mobile sources represent the largest contributor to air toxics, nationwide. Air toxics are pollutants known or suspected to cause cancer or other serious health or environmental effects.

Examples of toxic air pollutants include benzene, which is found in gasoline. Carbon monoxide—a poisonous gas—forms when carbon in fuel does not burn completely. The main source of carbon monoxide is vehicle emissions. In fact, according to the EPA, as much as 95% of the carbon monoxide in a typical U.S. city comes from mobile sources.

Hydrocarbon emissions also result from incomplete fuel combustion, and they are a precursor to ground-level ozone (which is a key component of smog). Today's cars are equipped with emission controls designed to reduce both exhaust and evaporative hydrocarbon emissions.

Nitrogen oxides form when fuel burns at high temperatures, such as in motor vehicle engines. Mobile sources are responsible for more than half of all nitrogen oxide emissions in the United States. Both on-road and off-road mobile sources are major nitrogen oxide polluters. Mobile source emissions also contain harmful particulate matter, and are given off by on-road and off-road vehicles. Diesel-powered vehicles and engines contribute more than half the mobile source particulate emissions.

According to the EPA, successful pollution solutions involve a variety of approaches. From better engine design to better transit options, experts believe programs to reduce mobile source pollution must address not only vehicles, engines, and equipment, but also the fuels they use and the people who operate them. This approach to mobile source emission control has greatly reduced air pollution during the past 30 years. Technological advances in vehicle and engine design, together with cleaner, higher-quality fuels, have helped reduce emissions.

THERMAL POLLUTION AND THE HEAT ISLAND EFFECT

Thermal pollution may be a problem where industrial sources use water as a coolant. These industries include conventional industry and coal-fired, oil-fired, or nuclear-powered electricity plants. Thermal pollution occurs when the temperature of the coolant water reaches the point where it can kill or harm fish or other wildlife. Thermal pollution results when water is used for absorbing heat and returned to a receiving stream before cooling down to normal stream temperature. This type of polluting discharge is regulated just as chemical pollutants are.

Other causes of thermal pollution include loss of tree coverage over a body of water because of logging or construction; damming of water, which then slows the water down and causes temperatures to increase; and increased turbidity, which adds more color to the water, causing more heat absorption.

According to the EPA, the major effect of thermal pollution is a reduction in the dissolved oxygen (DO) of a stream, which affects plant and animal life. Many species of fish cannot live in low oxygen streams. For example, most of the popular game fish, such as salmon or trout, need high oxygen levels (7 to 10 parts per million). Fish, such as catfish and carp, can tolerate lower oxygen levels (3 to 4.5 ppm). High temperatures and the resulting low oxygen also interfere with breeding activities and egg and larval development of many organisms.

The term *heat island* refers to urban air and surface temperatures that are higher than nearby rural areas. Many U.S. cities and suburbs have air temperatures up to 10°F (5.6°C) warmer than the surrounding natural land cover. When cities remove the natural vegetation, build roads, sidewalks, and other paved surfaces, it can cause the urban area to become hotter by:

- Lowering the natural cooling effect—By removing vegetation, the vegetation cannot "naturally"cool the air through natural shade and evaporation of water around it.
- Trapping heat—Tall buildings with narrow streets trap the hot air in them, warming the area up.
- Producing waste heat—Waste heat from vehicles, factories, air conditioners, and other equipment warms the surroundings, which then makes the heat island effect intensify.

Heat islands can occur all year long during the day or night. The temperature difference between urban and rural areas is usually greatest during calm, clear evenings. This is because rural areas cool off faster at night than cities, which retain much of the heat stored in roads, buildings, and other structures. As a result, the largest urban-rural temperature difference—or maximum heat island effect—occurs about three to five hours after sunset.

In the wintertime, some cities in cold climates may benefit from the warming effect of heat islands, because warmer temperatures can reduce heating energy needs and may help melt ice and snow on roads. In the summertime, however, the same city will experience the negative effects of the heat island: increased levels of air-conditioning demand, air pollution, greenhouse gas emissions, and heat-related illness and mortality, as well as discomfort.

Scientists believe that summertime heat islands may contribute to global warming because the demand for air conditioning is increasing. This results in additional power plant emissions of heat-trapping greenhouse gases. This is why it is important that strategies be designed to reduce heat islands, and to reduce the harmful emissions that contribute to global warming. Today, the EPA is involved in an extensive amount of research to better understand the impacts and provide communities with information to develop programs to deal with the issue.

The EPA has identified several ways to lessen the impacts of heat islands. These heat island reduction strategies include installing cool or vegetated green roofs; planting trees and vegetation; and switching to cool paving materials. Factors such as land-use patterns, materials used in road and building construction, and the coverage of urban trees and vegetation can be directly affected by decision makers. According to the EPA, this is where policies and programs to reduce the impacts of heat islands—and achieve related environmental and energy-savings goals—can be most effective.

Solutions used to date include the following:

- Cool roofs—More than 90% of the roofs in the United States are dark-colored. These low-reflectance surfaces reach temperatures of 150°F to 190°F (66°C to 88°C) and contribute to increased utility bills for air conditioning, reduced indoor comfort, increased air pollution, and faster deterioration of roofing materials. In contrast, cool roof systems with high reflectance and emittance stay up to 70°F (39°C) cooler than traditional materials during peak summer weather. Cool roofs are designed to reflect heat instead of absorb it. Benefits of cool roofs include reduced building heat-gain and savings on summertime air-conditioning bills. By minimizing energy use, cool roofs do more than save money—they reduce the demand for electric power and resulting air pollution and greenhouse gas emissions.
- Green roofs—Another alternative to traditional roofing materials is a rooftop garden, or "green roof." On hot summer days, the surface temperature of a vegetated rooftop can be cooler than the air temperature, whereas the surface of a traditional rooftop can be up to 90°F (50°C) warmer. A green roof consists of vegetation and

soil, or a growing medium, planted over a waterproofing layer. Additional layers, such as a root barrier and drainage and irrigation systems may also be included.

- Trees and vegetation—Planting trees and vegetation is a simple and effective way to reduce heat islands. Widespread planting in a city can decrease local surface and air temperatures. Strategic planting around homes and buildings directly cools the interior of homes and buildings, decreasing air-conditioning costs and peak energy demand.

- Cool pavements—There are some paving materials that lower surface temperature. Large parking areas, terminal facilities, airfields, or urban roadways with large expanses of paved surface are examples where cool pavements may be most practical. Cool paving materials have two key properties. They have high solar reflectance (so the heat does not absorb), and they are permeable so that the cooling effect of evaporation can occur.

ACID RAIN

Acid rain—as well as acid snow, acid fog or mist, acid gas, and acid dust—are all related air pollutants that can be harmful to people's and animals' health, cause hazy skies, and damage the environment. The 1990 Clean Air Act includes a program to reduce acid air pollution.

The pollutants that cause acid rain that have received the most attention come from big coal-burning power plants in the Midwest. These plants burn midwestern and Appalachian coal, some of which contains a lot of sulfur. Sulfur in coal becomes sulfur dioxide (SO_2) when coal is burned. Big power plants burn large quantities of coal, so they release large amounts of sulfur dioxide, as well as NO_x (nitrogen oxides). These are acidic chemicals, related to two strong acids: sulfuric acid and nitric acid.

The sulfur dioxide and nitrogen oxides released from the midwestern power plants rise high into the air and are carried by winds toward the East Coast of the United States and Canada. When winds blow the acid chemicals into areas where there is wet weather, the acids become part of the rain, snow, or fog. In areas where the weather is dry, the acid chemicals may fall to Earth in gases or dusts.

Lakes and streams are normally slightly **acidic**, but acid rain can make them very acidic. These conditions have the power to damage plant and animal life. It is also harmful to sensitive forest soils and trees. Heavy rainstorms and melting snow can cause temporary increases in acidity in lakes and streams. The pollutants that cause acid rain can make the air hazy or foggy.

Acid rain does more than environmental damage; it can damage health and property as well. According to the U.S. Environmental Protection Agency, acid air pollution has been linked to breathing and lung problems in children and in people who have asthma. Even healthy people can have their lungs damaged by acid air pollutants. It can also eat away stone buildings and statues, harming historical landmarks.

In an attempt to control acid rain, the EPA has put programs into effect to reduce, over a period of years, the emissions that are key components of acid rain. Scientists believe that reducing sulfur dioxide releases should cause a major reduction in acid rain over the next few years. Reducing nitrogen oxide releases will reduce both acid rain and smog formation.

INDOOR AIR POLLUTION

Since most people spend a majority of their lives indoors, the quality of indoor air is a major area of concern for the EPA. Sources of indoor air pollution include oil, gas, kerosene, coal, wood, tobacco products, and household cleaning products. Building materials and furnishings such as asbestos-containing insulation, damp carpets, and lead-based paints can also cause indoor air pollution. It is important to everyone's health to monitor and improve the quality of air in homes, schools, and offices. Items in particular that need to be controlled include mold, radon, tobacco, smoke, pesticides, asbestos, lead, biological contaminants, and formaldehyde.

A number of well-identified illnesses, such as Legionnaires' disease, asthma, hypersensitivity pneumonitis, and humidifier fever, have been directly traced to specific building problems. These are called building-related illnesses. Most of these diseases can be treated but pose serious risks and need immediate attention.

Some health specialists have identified a syndrome associated with indoor air pollution, called "Sick Building Syndrome" (SBS). SBS is used to describe situations in which building occupants experience acute health and comfort effects that appear to be linked to time spent in a building, but no specific illness or cause can be identified. The complaints may be localized in a particular room or zone, or may be widespread throughout the building.

A 1984 World Health Organization Committee report suggested that up to 30% of new and remodeled buildings worldwide may be the subject of excessive complaints related to indoor air quality. Indicators of SBS include symptoms associated with acute discomfort, such as headache; eye, nose, or throat irritation; dry cough; dry or itchy skin; dizziness and nausea; difficulty in concentrating; fatigue; and sensitivity to odors. In addition, most of the complainants report relief soon after leaving the building. It is believed that the following factors may cause the syndrome:

- Inadequate ventilation
- Chemical contaminants from indoor sources (adhesives, carpeting, copy machines, cleaning agents)
- Chemical contaminants from outdoor sources (motor vehicle exhausts, plumbing vents, and building exhausts)
- Biological contaminants (bacteria, mold, pollen, and viruses)

Maintaining high-quality air indoors and out is important in order to maintain good health and a healthy environment.

CONSERVATION OF WATER AND ATMOSPHERIC RESOURCES

A responsible way to manage water and atmospheric resources is through conservation. This chapter will look at important conservation issues. It will examine effective water conservation practices, preservation of delicate coral reef systems, preserving the ecosystem of frozen Antarctica, and repairing the ozone layer.

WATER CONSERVATION

On the average, every American uses about 150 gallons (568 l) of water each day. Of this amount, only one-half gallon (1.9 l) is used for actual drinking water. The other 149.5 gallons (566 l) goes for cleaning, watering the lawn, cooking, flushing the toilet, washing cars, bathing, brushing teeth, rinsing food, washing dishes, laundry, and many other uses. One efficient way to reduce water pollution is to simply reduce water consumption. Wastewater treatment plant operators report that they treat millions of gallons of water that does not need treatment to begin with.

Effective personal water conservation can be accomplished by changing a few habits. According to the U.S. Environmental Protection Agency (EPA), 2 gallons (7.6 l) of water can be saved every minute if fruits and vegetables are peeled before being washed. Using a dishwasher uses less water than washing by hand. A standard dishwasher uses less than 6 gallons (23 l) a load, while washing by hand and leaving the water running can use many more gallons. Washing full loads of laundry instead of many partial loads also saves gallons of water. Oftentimes, hotels in drought-stricken areas will post a sign encouraging guests to conserve water.

Water conservation is the most cost-effective and environmentally sound way to reduce the demand for water, because it stretches supplies further. Using less water also puts less pressure on sewage treatment facilities, and uses less energy for water heating.

There are many effective ways to conserve water at home. New washing machines can reduce water consumption by one-third, or more than 400 gallons a month (1,514 l) for a family of four. The most water use occurs in the bathroom. Simply turning off the water when brushing your teeth could save as much as 3 gallons (11.4 l) per person per day. Taking a shower instead of a bath can save up to 25 gallons (95 l), and low-flow showerheads can reduce consumption even more.

If taking a shower, do not waste cold water while waiting for hot water to reach the showerhead. Catch that water in a container to use on your outside plants or to flush your toilet. According to the Metropolitan Water District of Southern California, this can save 200 to 300 gallons (757 to 1,136 l) each month.

Keep a bottle of drinking water in the refrigerator, instead of running the tap water until it gets cold. When cooking, do not defrost frozen foods with running water. Either plan ahead by placing frozen items in the refrigerator overnight or defrost them in the microwave. This can save 50 to 150 gallons (189 to 568 l) each month. Do not let the faucet run while cleaning vegetables. Instead, rinse them in a filled sink or pan. This saves 150 to 250 gallons (568 to 946 l) a month. Use the garbage disposal less, which can save 50 to 150 gallons (189 to 568 l) a month.

A large percentage of the water used each day is for flushing toilets. New toilets use less than one-third the water of older models. Older toilets, however, can still work effectively with less water. Devices, such as toilet dams, block part of the water in the tank and reduce the amount used with each flush. The same effect can also be achieved by putting a water-filled plastic bottle in the toilet tank. This displaces the water, which means less of it is used. People commonly place a brick in the toilet tank, but this is not recommended, because it can break apart and clog the water pipes over time.

Another water-saving practice is to repair leaks in pipes immediately. Even a small drip can waste hundreds of gallons of water a day and add to the treatment loads of sewer or septic systems. Washing the car with a running hose will use more than 100 gallons (379 l) of water. Using a bucket and sponge cuts that by 90%.

In some circumstances, gray water can be reused. "Gray water" is wastewater collected from clothes washers, bathtubs, showers, laundry, and bathroom sinks. If it is properly collected and stored, it can be safely reused. This reduces freshwater consumption. Gray water is distinguished from "black water," which is wastewater from toilets, kitchen sinks, and dishwashers. Black water should never be reused in the home because of possible contamination by bacteria, viruses, and other pathogens.

Gray water does not require extensive chemical or biological treatment before being used for landscape irrigation. Gray water can be put to uses such as landscaping and to irrigate trees—just not on food plants (especially those eaten raw, such as carrots, tomatoes, or lettuce). If using gray water that contains detergents (such as from the washing machine) special detergents can be purchased to lessen any harmful impacts on plants.

Water can also be conserved in outdoor uses. For instance, it is always more efficient to water the yard in the early morning or at night when the sun will not cause as much evaporation. If yards are watered during the hottest part of the day, a large share of it evaporates and is wasted. Watering lawns and plants early in the morning is even better in order to prevent the growth of fungus.

For residents with swimming pools, a pool cover should be used when the pool is not occupied in order to cut down on evaporation. This also keeps the pool cleaner and reduces the need to add chemicals. This can save 1,000 gallons (3,785 l) a month.

Lawns should not be watered on windy days because the wind causes too much evaporation. This practice is extremely inefficient because it wastes up to 300 gallons (1,136 l) in one watering. Watering should also be decreased on cool, overcast days, or rainy days. This can save up to 300 gallons (1,136 l) each time. Lawn mower blades should be set one notch higher than usual. When grass is allowed to grow longer, less water evaporates. This can save 500 to 1,500 gallons (1,893 to 5,678 l) each month.

When washing a car, it is wise to park the car on a lawn. The rinse water can help water the grass. If a car is taken to a car wash, visit one that recycles its wash water. It is also important to dispose of hazardous materials properly. One quart of oil can contaminate 250,000 gallons (946,353 l) of water, which then cannot be used for other freshwater demands. It is important to remember that people live downstream from you and the pollution you put in the water impacts their fresh-water supply.

Children should not play with garden hoses. This can save 10 gallons (38 l) a minute. If children want to play in the sprinklers, it should only be done while actually watering the lawn.

It is also possible to collect rainwater for watering the yard. Runoff from rain gutters can be redirected with tubing attached to down-spouts, which then channel it to planted areas. An added benefit of rainwater harvesting is that plants thrive on it. Rainwater is very low in salts, and directing runoff to plants can help leach out salts that accumulate from irrigation. Also, the lightning in thunderstorms creates a beneficial form of nitrogen, which the rain washes out of the air, which is then delivered to plants for their growth.

Clean water is essential to the health of all forms of wildlife. If water is polluted, it can kill wildlife. Some conservation preserves are established in order to provide cleaner environments to indigenous animals. *(Photo courtesy of Nature's Images)*

The following list illustrates more ways water can be conserved:

- Keep showers to under five minutes.
- Only use a little water in the bathtub—do not fill it all the way up.
- Flush the toilet only when necessary (do not use it to flush tissues, spiders, cigarettes, or anything else it was not intended for).
- Use a turn-off nozzle on the end of the hose to adjust the water flow and turn the water off and on, rather than using a hose that runs continually.

Keeping oceans clean creates healthy environments for both ocean and coastal life. Keeping beaches pristine also promotes tourism and a healthy economy. This rugged volcanic coast is on the island of Kauai, Hawaii. *(Photo courtesy of Nature's Images)*

- Turn the water faucet off tightly—drips add up.
- Put water in the kitchen sink to wash and rinse dishes.
- Put unused drinking-water ice cubes on indoor plants.
- When washing your hands, do not let the water run while you lather.
- Do not use recreational water toys that require a constant flow of water in order to operate.

When water is treated properly and conserved, more clean water is available. When healthy conservation practices are followed, it also benefits wildlife in outdoor natural settings.

Clean water for the environment is achieved through pollution control, effective water management, and appropriate land management (such as keeping eroded soil out of water sources).

Technology also contributes to water conservation through the development of water-saving devices. For example, there are instant hot water devices, which have a recirculation system that uses a pump at a home's water heater to keep the line hot and comfortable from the moment the water is turned on, eliminating the need to run the water until it heats up. Leak detection equipment has also been developed, which can continuously monitor a plumbing system for leaks. Easily installed on pipe fittings, they are held in place by a strong magnet and have a battery life of up to 10 years; they also require no maintenance. Smart irrigation controllers have been developed to reduce outdoor water use by monitoring conditions, soil moisture, and plant type and then applying just the right amount of water required.

Pre-rinse spray valves have been developed for uses in restaurants in order to cut down the amount of water needed to rinse dishes. Vertical stop sprinkler heads shut off all water flow when the water is not in use. A special water broom has been developed for outdoor use. By combining air and water pressure, this tool cleans and removes dirt, dust, food spills, leaves, litter, sawdust, and bird droppings from concrete, asphalt, and other surfaces.

CORAL REEF PRESERVATION

Coral reefs are some of the oldest and most diverse ecosystems on Earth. They provide resources and services worth many billions of dollars each year. Millions of people and thousands of communities all over the world depend on coral reefs for food, protection, and jobs. In 2000, the U.S. Government put the Coral Reef Conservation Act into effect, to protect the health and future of coral reefs.

Coral reefs are critical to preserve because they provide a home for about one million species, including fish, corals, lobsters, clams, seahorses, sponges, sea turtles, and eels, to name a few of the wildlife species that rely on reefs for their survival.

Coral reefs provide habitat for many species. This green turtle swims along the reef in the Florida Keys National Marine Sanctuary. *(Photo courtesy of National Oceanic and Atmospheric Administration; photo by Commander Alan Bunn, NOAA Corps (ret.), Coral Kingdom Collection)*

Today, these important habitats are threatened by a variety of human activities. Many of the world's reefs have already been destroyed or severely damaged by water pollution, overfishing and destructive fishing practices, disease, global climate change, and ship groundings. By taking action now, however, these reefs can be preserved.

Healthy coral reefs support a thriving tourism industry. Every year, millions of scuba divers, snorkelers, and fishermen visit coral reefs to enjoy their abundant sea life. Despite their great economic and recreational value, coral reefs are severely threatened by pollution, disease, and habitat destruction. Once coral reefs are damaged, they negatively impact the natural balance that has been established over a long period

An eel guards his home in a coral reef within the Gulf of Aqaba, Red Sea. *(Photo courtesy of National Oceanic and Atmospheric Administration; photo by Mohammed Al Momany, Aqaba, Jordan; Coral Kingdom Collection)*

of time. They are less able to support the many creatures that inhabit them, and when a coral reef supports fewer fish, plants, and animals, it also loses value as a tourist destination.

Coral reefs are sometimes considered by researchers to be the "medicine cabinets" of the twenty-first century. Coral reef plants and animals are important sources of new medicines being developed to treat many medical conditions, such as cancer, arthritis, human bacterial infections, heart disease, viruses, and other diseases. Some scientists are studying organisms in coral reefs that produce chemical substances designed to protect them by repelling predators. Researchers are looking into these capabilities in the hope that there may be some

Things You Can Do to Protect Coral Reefs

Even if you do not live near a reef, you can help protect coral reefs by doing the following things:

- Educate yourself about coral reefs and the habitats they support.

- Make sure that sewage from your home is correctly treated.

- Support organizations that protect coral reefs.

- Volunteer to participate in a reef cleanup.

- Only buy marine fish and other reef organisms when you know they have been collected in an ecologically sound manner.

- Find out what aquariums and zoos in your community are doing to conserve coral reefs, and volunteer to help.

- If you scuba dive, never touch the coral. Contact can hurt you and will damage the delicate coral animals. Stay off the bottom because disturbed sediments can smother the corals.

- Support reef-friendly businesses that are concerned about taking care of coral reefs.

- Recycle—this helps keep garbage from being dumped in the oceans.

- Conserve water to cut back wastewater being drained into the ocean.

- Report illegal dumping into waterways.

- When boating, never anchor on the reef. If you are boating near a coral reef, use mooring buoy systems when they are available.

- Stay informed and help educate others.

Source: National Oceanic and Atmospheric Administration

medicinal benefits for humans. Similar to today's rain forests, many experts believe coral reefs may be an important source of new medicines, nutritional supplements, and many other useful products.

Coral reef structures also perform beneficial functions for the environment. They buffer shorelines against waves, storms, and floods, which helps to prevent loss of life, property damage, and erosion. When reefs are damaged or destroyed, the absence of this natural barrier can increase the damage to coastal communities from normal wave action and violent storms, because the coasts must then face the brunt of the storm's energy. Several million people live in U.S. coastal areas adjacent to, or near, coral reefs. While some coastal development is required to provide coastal residents with basic necessities, the impacts of excessive coastal development (such as marinas, dock and bridge construction, and dredging to replenish beaches) and polluted runoff from coastal areas can ultimately damage coral reefs if they are not controlled. Therefore, the health of coral reefs depends on sustainable coastal development practices that protect sensitive coral ecosystems and the creatures that reside there.

PRESERVING ANTARCTICA

Antarctica—a unique environment—is an area that scientists from around the world visit to study the frozen landscape and the wildlife that inhabits it. For example, a team of scientists from the University of Nebraska–Lincoln are currently in Antarctica investigating the continent's role in global climate change. They are collecting geological data by drilling and recovering rock core samples from the McMurdo Sound region. Their research goal is to develop a detailed history of the Antarctic climate and the expansion and contraction of the Ross Sea area's ice sheets over the past 20 million years. This will provide important data about Antarctica's role in global climate change.

Antarctica and the surrounding area are natural laboratories for scientific research that cannot be done anywhere else on Earth. Among the unusual aspects of the continent are its harsh climate and extremely cold, ice-filled oceans; vast polar ice cap and large glaciers; geologic formations and structures that are related to more northerly land masses; uniquely adapted forms of plant and animal life; and unusual meteorological phenomena. This diversity has attracted exploration and scientific curiosity for more than a hundred years. It is a desirable place for meteorologists, **oceanographers**, atmospheric physicists, geologists, glaciologists, seismologists, geophysicists, biologists, zoologists, and even the people from the medical community who are examining the effects of the Antarctic environment on human physiology. This research, involving so many disciplines, is carried out by scientists among the faculty and students of colleges and universities, government agencies, and private industry.

Antarctica is an ideal place to solve global scientific issues. For instance, the polar regions have been called Earth's window to outer space. With the discovery of polar stratospheric ozone depletions, the ultraviolet window previously thought "closed" is now known to "open" in certain seasons. Current research focuses on stratospheric chemistry, aerosols, and the vital role played by ozone.

Antarctica is also an astronomer's dream come true. The Amundsen–Scott South Pole Station is one of the best places on Earth to study the stars. Observers there take advantage of the unique characteristics of the South Pole to study the evolution and structure of the universe.

Conditions on the frozen Antarctic surface are so harsh that few life-forms survive year-round above the ice. Of particular interest to biologists are the McMurdo Dry Valleys, which represent a region where life approaches its environmental limits in the harsh elements.

Researchers say much of the story of Antarctica is written beneath the ice in the rocks that make up about 9% of Earth's continental crust. Geologic evidence indicates that at one time the continent had a temperate climate and was part of an ancient, considerably larger landmass, known as Gondwanaland.

An ice sheet covers all but 2.4% of Antarctica's 5.4 million square miles (14 million sq. km). This ice contains 70% of all the world's freshwater. In order to predict the ice sheet's future behavior and its effect on global climate, glaciologists must have a thorough understanding of its history, current state, and internal dynamics.

The South Pole offers a unique location for scientists to pursue new discoveries and increase scientific knowledge. Found only in Antarctica, these Emperor penguins live in the Southwest Ross Sea area. *(Photo courtesy of the National Oceanic and Atmospheric Administration, Photographer: Michael Van Woert, NOAA Corps Collection)*

The weather systems that constantly circle Antarctica drive storms across the Southern Ocean and beyond, while the seasonal formation and melting of sea ice has an important effect on the world's weather. Antarctic stations collect daily meteorological observations and broadcast them to surrounding countries to help in weather forecasting.

The Antarctic Convergence divides the cold southern water masses from the warmer northern waters, creating the world's largest current flowing at an average speed of half a knot eastward around the continent. In addition, sea ice forms outward up to 932 miles (1,500 km) from the continent every winter. Oceanographic studies focus on these two interrelated phenomena and their effects on both marine ecosystems and Earth's climate patterns.

REPAIRING THE OZONE LAYER

Scientists have found holes in the ozone layer high above the Earth. Ozone holes are not just empty spaces in the sky. They are much like the worn-out places in a blanket: There are still threads covering the worn-out area, but the fabric can be so thin that you can see right through it. The 1990 Clean Air Act has provisions for fixing the holes, but repairs will take a long time.

Ozone in the stratosphere—the layer of the atmosphere 9 to 31 miles (14 to 50 km) above the Earth—serves as a protective shield, filtering out harmful sun rays, including a type of sunlight called ultraviolet B. Exposure to ultraviolet B has been linked to development of cataracts (eye damage) and skin cancer.

In the mid-1970s, scientists suggested that **chlorofluorocarbons (CFCs)** could destroy stratospheric ozone. CFCs were widely used then as aerosol propellants in consumer products such as hairsprays and deodorants, and for many other uses in industry. Because of concern about the possible effects of CFCs on the ozone layer, the U.S. government banned CFCs as propellants in aerosol cans in 1978.

Since the aerosol ban, scientists have continued to measure the ozone layer. A few years ago, an ozone hole was found above Antarctica, including the area of the South Pole. This hole, which has been appearing each year during the Antarctic winter, is bigger in area than the continental United States. Another thin spot in the ozone layer has also been discovered in the Northern Hemisphere, straddling portions of the United States, Canada, and the Arctic. Initially, the hole was detected only in winter and spring, but more recently has continued into summer. Between 1978 and 1991, there was a 4% to 5% loss of ozone in the stratosphere over the United States—which represents a significant loss. Ozone holes have also been found recently over northern Europe. There is also evidence that holes in the ozone layer damage plant life. Scientists are looking into possible harm to agriculture, as well.

Because of this threat to the ozone layer, 93 nations—including the United States—have jointly agreed to reduce their production and use of ozone-destroying chemicals. When researchers discovered that the ozone layer was thinning more quickly than first thought, this agreement was revised to speed up the phase-out of the use of ozone-destroying chemicals.

Unfortunately, this problem does not have an easy fix. It will be a long time before the ozone layer will be repaired. Because of the ozone-destroying chemicals already in the stratosphere and those that will arrive within the next few years, experts warn that ozone destruction will probably continue for another 20 years. As substitutes are developed for ozone-destroying substances, the EPA must determine that these replacements will be safe for human health and the environment before they can be produced and sold. These substances take time to test and verify.

Conservation of all atmospheric and water resources is important to the future of life on Earth. As technology continues to advance and scientists learn more, better conservation techniques will be developed.

CONCLUSION: THE FUTURE OF WATER AND ATMOSPHERE

This chapter looks to the future of water and atmospheric resources. It focuses specifically on the global challenges that currently face society, the ocean's resources, and why many scientists refer to the oceans as the Earth's "final frontier"—and what the focus will be regarding future research for these resources.

GLOBAL CHALLENGES

Today, many experts believe the oceans and the life they support are under threat. In some areas, sewage and industrial waste are being dumped and poured from pipelines into the oceans. Carrying chemicals and metals, the pollutants entering the ocean can have a disastrous effect on the food chain. Oil spills, as already mentioned, smother marine life and do great damage. Garbage dumped into the ocean can also be deadly. For example, turtles mistake plastic bags for jellyfish and eat them; and abandoned fishing nets entangle sea birds and sea mammals, such as dolphins, and submerge and drown them. Overharvesting has depleted many forms of ocean life. Many species of marine creatures have become endangered and are now rare because so many have been killed for sport. Tropical islands and coasts with coral reefs attract huge numbers of tourists every year, who have unfortunately taken a toll on ocean habitat, disrupting the natural life cycles of marine life. Corals and shellfish are destroyed by heavy boat anchors and by divers hunting for souvenirs.

At the same time, pollutants from automobiles, power plants, industry, and other sources are being spewed into the atmosphere at alarming rates, causing long-term detrimental effects to our quality of life and the climate.

One thing is certain—this is a global problem. The atmosphere and oceans know no boundaries. It will take the cooperation and efforts of all the countries of the world to share ocean and atmospheric resources fairly and to make laws that will prevent overfishing, pollution, and other environmental impacts. This will not be an easy task; it is often difficult for countries to agree on the best way of doing things. It is also hard to get people to obey laws when the oceans and atmosphere are so vast and difficult to patrol or monitor. The work of oceanographers, meteorologists, climatologists, and mathematical modelers is vital if humans are to decide how to best manage these precious resources now and in the future, because they truly are the lifeblood of all living systems.

OCEAN RESOURCES—THE EARTH'S FINAL FRONTIER

Because relatively little exploration has occurred at deep-ocean depths, the ocean is considered, by many scientists, to be the Earth's "final frontier." A wide variety of mineral resources are found on the seafloor. These resources fall into four general categories:

- Granular sediments
- Placer minerals
- Hydrothermal deposits
- Hydrogenetic minerals

Granular sediments are eroded particles weathered on land and carried by rivers or glaciers and deposited in the oceans. The sediment deposits are stratified by size—the heaviest particles settle out first; the finest grains settle out last. Sediments can include gravel, sand, silt, and clay. Placer minerals can be deposits of gold, platinum, titanium, tin, and diamonds, as well as heavy minerals and ores. Hydrothermal minerals are those associated with volcanic activity. These include sulfide deposits rich in copper, zinc, lead, gold, and silver. Hydrogenetic deposits are precipitated from seawater, and include minerals such as phosphorite, salt, barite, and iron-manganese nodules, and crusts rich in cobalt, platinum, nickel, copper, and rare earth elements.

The Outer Continental Shelf (OCS) of the United States is a significant source of oil and gas for the nation's energy supply. For example, by the end of 2002, U.S. offshore sources supplied more than 25% of the country's natural gas production and more than 30% of total domestic oil production. Many experts feel there are a lot of deposits that have not been discovered yet: There could be up to 76 billion barrels of oil and 406.1 trillion cubic feet (11.5 trillion cubic meters) of gas. These volumes represent about 60% of the oil and 41% of the natural gas resources estimated to be contained in remaining undiscovered fields in the United States. The principal economically recoverable mineral resources of the ocean include salt; potassium; magnesium; sand and gravel; limestone and gypsum; manganese nodules; phosphorites; metal deposits associated with volcanism and seafloor vents; placer gold, tin, titanium, and diamonds; and water itself.

There is so much salt stored in the oceans that scientists believe it could supply all human needs for thousands of years. Although salt is extracted directly from the oceans in many countries by evaporating the water and leaving the residual salts, most of the nearly 200 million metric tons of salt produced annually are mined from large beds of salt. These beds, which are now deeply buried, were left when waters from ancient oceans evaporated in shallow seas, leaving thick beds of salt. The beds were subsequently covered and protected from being dissolved and destroyed.

Potassium salts, which occur along common salt, can also be mined. These deposits are large enough to yield tens of millions of metric tons each year.

Magnesium is the only metal directly extracted from seawater. The majority of magnesium metal and many of the magnesium salts produced in the United States are extracted from seawater electrolytically.

Sand and gravel are a key mineral resource found in the ocean. The **ocean basins** constitute the ultimate depositional site of sediments eroded from the land, and beaches represent the largest residual deposits of sand. Although beaches and nearshore sediments are locally extracted for use in construction, they are usually considered too valuable as recreational areas to permit removal for construction purposes. Older beach sand deposits that have lost their recreational value, however, are often mined for construction materials, glass manufacture, and for preparation of silicon metal. Gravel deposits are utilized extensively for building materials.

The continents and tropical islands contain vast deposits of limestone that are extensively mined. Most of the limestone is used directly in cut or crushed form, but some is also calcined (cooked) to be converted into cement used for construction purposes. Gypsum forms during the evaporation of seawater and can occur with evaporite salts near limestone. Gypsum deposits are mined and converted into plaster of Paris and used for construction.

Manganese nodules have received a lot of attention recently as a valuable mineral resource. The deep-ocean floor contains extremely large quantities of nodules, usually about the size of a potato. Although commonly called manganese nodules, they usually contain more iron than manganese, but do constitute the largest known resource of manganese. These small, dark, and round nodules contain manganese, nickel, copper, cobalt, and other minerals. They are found along the floor of the Atlantic and Pacific oceans. Steel production, which requires millions of tons of manganese annually, is looking toward manganese nodules as an important resource. Though ocean mining for manganese nodules has generated a great deal of interest, several factors have stood in the way, such as the difficult ocean terrain, the high cost, and political and international difficulties relating to its legality. Nevertheless, these rich deposits are considered a potential resource for the future.

Phosphorites are another important mineral resource from the ocean. Phosphate-rich crusts and granules exist in shallow marine environments. According to experts, they represent future potential reserves if land-based deposits become depleted.

Submarine investigations of oceanic rift zones have revealed that rich deposits of zinc and copper, with associated lead, silver, and gold, are forming at the sites of hot hydrothermal features commonly called **black smokers**. These metal-rich deposits, ranging from chimney- to pancake-like, form where deeply circulating seawater has dissolved metals from the underlying rocks. These deposits issue out onto the cold seafloor along major fractures. The deposits forming today are not being mined because of their remote locations.

Deep-sea **hydrothermal vents** support extraordinary ecosystems deep beneath the surface of the oceans. These unique ecosystems are the only communities on Earth whose immediate energy source is not sunlight. The living organisms at the hydrothermal vents also play an important role in the formation of the sulfide chimney structures—a unique combination of biology and chemistry. Scientists believe that by understanding this biochemical mineral formation process, it will help them to better understand mineral ore formation processes in general.

Placer deposits of gold, tin, titanium, and diamonds are also found in the ocean. Placer deposits are mineral deposits formed by the weathering, movement, deposition, and concentration of particles. The mineral concentrated is usually a heavy mineral, such as gold. Today, a substantial amount of the world's tin and many of its gem diamonds are recovered by dredging nearshore ocean sediments for minerals that were carried into the sea by rivers. Gold has been recovered in the past from such deposits, such as the rich deposits that have historically been recovered in Nome, Alaska. Large quantities of placer titanium minerals also occur in beach and sediments near the shores. Mining today,

The blackened water is jetting out at 3.3 to 16 feet (1 to 5 m) per second from this black smoker, which is more than 700°F (380°C) hotter than a pizza oven. *(Courtesy NOAA, courtesy of Spiess, Macdonald, et al., 1980)*

The animals that live by hydrothermal vents include tube worms, clams, and crabs. These life forms do not need sunlight to survive. *(Courtesy NOAA, from Macdonald and Lyendyk,* Scientific American, *1981)*

however, is concentrated mostly to the beaches of onshore deposits because it is still very expensive to mine in deeper locations in the ocean. There are also environmental concerns that need to be resolved, such as disruption of delicate marine ecosystems.

The world's oceans, with a total volume of more than 119,956,379 cubic miles (500 million cubic kilometers), contain more than 97% of all the water on Earth. It is unusable for most human needs, however, because of its high salt content (3.5%). The technology to extract freshwater from ocean water has been in existence for quite some time, but it is very expensive, so it is still a relatively uncommon practice. Technological advances, especially in reverse osmosis, are continuing

Submersibles are used to explore the depths of oceans. Usually quite small and confined, they operate under enormous pressures and must supply their own light in order to see. *(Photo courtesy NOAA)*

to increase the efficiency of freshwater extraction, so that some day in the future it will become more feasible.

Many scientists believe we are facing the beginning of a new age of discovery—that of deep-ocean mining. Dr. Steven Scott, a geologist at the University of Toronto, in Toronto, Canada, says that advances in marine geology and deep-ocean technology have combined to make it realistic to go more than 1.2 miles (2 km) underwater for mineral resources.

Scott believes the key challenge for new marine mining companies will be developing the technology to extract the ore from the extreme depths. He envisions the use of "deep-sea versions of robotic coal-mining machines" with the ore piped up to mining ships, or semisubmersible platforms, like those used by the offshore oil industry.

As deep-sea technology progresses, submersibles will be further refined and improved in order to explore the oceans for minerals. Currently, an underwater mining vehicle capable of mining and pumping sand from the ocean floor through a flexible riser system has been developed as the first step toward technology for deep-sea mining.

FUTURE RESEARCH

The principal areas of research—now and in the future—are in the fields of ocean, lake, and coastal research; weather and air-quality research; and climate research.

Ocean, Lake, and Coastal Research

Scientists are only beginning to understand how unique the oceans are. More than a century of oceanographic research by the U.S. National Oceanic and Atmospheric Administration (NOAA) has revealed that oceans play a critical role in regulating the Earth's weather and climate. They provide habitat for an extraordinarily diverse community of plants and animals, provide useful food and medicines, and significantly influence the creation of the coastlines and their constantly evolving shape. However, scientists believe we are still in the infancy of understanding this enormous resource, but they also believe that knowledge of the oceans, their resources, and their relationship to human activities, is vital to society and to the Earth's existence.

NOAA research, in cooperation with many other research partners (from private and educational organizations) is taking the lead on exploring and investigating habitats and resources. Researchers are focusing on water resources and **hydrology**, ocean exploration and underwater research, habitat protection and restoration, the threat of aquatic invasive species, ecological forecasting, hurricanes and coastal management, fisheries and aquaculture, and marine biotechnology.

According to the National Oceanic and Atmospheric Administration, the quantity and quality of water resources has been, and will continue to be, critically important in the future to ensure protection of life and property, economic well-being, and healthy coastal ecosystems. Because of the delicate balance of climate and the alarming decline in water supplies in certain drought-stricken regions, protecting and preserving vital water resources in the future will depend largely on sound management decisions supported by an in-depth, reliable scientific knowledge base. Key to this base is the full understanding of the hydrological cycle—the natural process by which water circulates among air, land, and water. Scientists are using hydrology, a scientific assessment of the volume, location and movement of water, to build complex mathematical models to understand the intricacies of this vital cycle. As technology progresses, scientists will be able to advance their knowledge of these critical resources.

The National Severe Storms Laboratory (NSSL) is working on computer programming that can provide information on flash flooding, river flooding, and agricultural and water resources management applications worldwide using radar data, satellite imagery, lightning strike data, rain gauge data, and surface and upper air observations. In ocean exploration and undersea research, scientists are involved in developing new technologies, ocean-floor mapping, coral study, and exploration of hydrothermal vents. New approaches, such as advanced seafloor observatories and human-occupied habitats, will provide priceless opportunities for long-term monitoring and study. Ships, submersibles, new diving technologies, and observation tools allow researchers to examine the oceans in systematic, scientific, and noninvasive ways, further protecting the environment.

A primary product of exploration is new and improved maps that characterize ocean regions and document the physical, biological, geological, chemical, and archaeological aspects of the ocean. Dense collections of corals found in dark, frigid waters provide habitat for diverse organisms, including fish and invertebrate communities. Like trees, corals add annual growth rings that are important indicators of past climates. Deep-sea coral ecosystems provide a rich biodiversity that may be a future source of innovative bio-compounds for development by pharmaceutical and biotechnology industries.

More than 70% of the Earth's volcanic activity takes place beneath the ocean's surface, where it has an impact on deep-ocean mixing, the global chemical and heat balance, and ancient biological communities. NOAA research utilizes exploration, long-term time series observations, remote monitoring, and innovative oceanographic instrumentation to look at effects on the oceans of deep-sea volcanoes and hydrothermal systems.

Habitat protection and restoration is actively going on in many parts of the world. For example, the Everglades/Florida Bay coastal ecosystem is being studied in order to predict the consequences of upstream restoration activities. NOAA is currently conducting biological, chemical, and physical studies to better understand the issues at hand. By understanding, protecting, and restoring habitats, it will be possible to have sustainable marine habitat in the future.

Aquatic invasive species (AIS) pose an increasing threat to the health of marine ecosystems. Researchers at NOAA are working to protect, restore, and manage the use of ocean, coastal, and lake resources and the environmental impacts resulting from aquatic invasions.

AIS are aquatic and terrestrial organisms and plants that have been introduced into new ecosystems throughout the United States and the world and are both harming the natural resources in these ecosystems and threatening the human use of these resources. Invasive

Healthy reef habitats have a tremendous aesthetic value. Proper care of their environment will ensure that they survive for centuries to come. *(Photo courtesy NOAA)*

species can enter the ocean from the ballast water of oceangoing ships, intentional and accidental releases of aquaculture species, aquarium specimens or bait, and other means. Foreign invaders, like the green crab, zebra mussel, and Pacific jellyfish, have displaced native species and diminished biodiversity, resulting in huge economic impacts and disruptions of ecosystems.

NOAA is currently involved in programs for invasive species prevention, monitoring, control, education, and research to prevent introduction and dispersal of aquatic invasive species. They are researching not only issues of prevention, but also monitoring early detection and rapid response. Restoring ecosystems is critical in order to prevent reinfestation of invasive species. Research is needed to improve understanding of the biology of invasive species and their effects on habitats, and to improve development of new restoration tools.

With advancements in observing and forecasting technology, NOAA is developing its capability to observe entire ecosystems and to predict ecosystem-wide changes before they occur. Observations of current conditions can be used to understand the Earth's climate system, global carbon cycle, global water cycle, nutrient pollution cycle, the multiplying effect of many stresses on an ecosystem, and the impacts of increased land use around coastal regions. NOAA is currently a leader in the effort to consolidate existing systems with multiple purposes into a more efficient, coordinated global observing system. This way, data collected by individual scientists can be merged with other collected data, making research much more efficient and productive. The most significant application of this data is for input into forecast models used to predict changes in global weather, climate, ocean, and ecosystem patterns.

Rather than just being used to forecast physical conditions, such as temperature or precipitation, biological, chemical, and physical data are now being integrated to produce whole ecosystem forecasts to predict outbreaks of potentially damaging environmental conditions before they occur. Examples of ecological predictions that are currently, or may soon be, produced by NOAA include climate impacts on ecosystems, coastal hazards predictions, and coral reef-bleaching predictions.

NOAA is also conducting research aimed at improved understanding and forecasts of hurricanes and other tropical systems. Their Tsunami Research Program is an integrated approach toward improved tsunami warning for Alaska, Hawaii, and the west coast of the United States.

Research is also ongoing to help understand and manage ocean, coastal, and lake fisheries resources. Many of these resources are in need of regeneration following years of excessive harvesting and the degradation of their environments from both natural and human-induced causes.

NOAA's interest in agriculture is to establish an environmentally sustainable, profitable, offshore aquaculture industry that will alleviate stress on natural fish stocks, create thousands of jobs, provide healthy protein to Americans at a reasonable cost, and improve food safety and security. They are involved in education and outreach activities that involve creating controlled spawning of fish species that could not be cultured before.

Marine biotechnology is the use of organisms, or their components, to provide goods or services. This area holds significant promise in improving human lives. NOAA's research in biotechnology is focused on therapeutic and industrial applications. For example, researchers are looking into developments of new anticancer drugs from marine invertebrates and genetically engineered microbes for use in oil spill cleanup. They are also looking at the development of synthetic antifreeze, water-resistant adhesives, and superabsorbent materials obtained from the proteins contained in various marine organisms. They are also studying the genetic engineering of marsh plants to create salt-tolerant crops and pursuing molecular research targeted at combating shipworms, corrosion, and other problems.

To date, researchers have mined a wealth of natural compounds found in marine organisms and discovered many with potential for use as life-saving drugs. Many scientists compare the potential of the world's oceans to the wealth of resources in the world's tropical rain forests. They believe as they explore further, they will find vast, untapped resources to prolong human life and increase the standard of living. For example, a compound derived from mangrove tunicates holds promise as a potent antitumor treatment; those from corals have potent anticancer activity. To conserve limited marine resources, researches are also developing ways to synthesize these products.

Weather and Air Quality Research

Observing the weather is not new; people have been observing it for thousands of years. Even so, little was understood about the complex atmospheric phenomena that create weather until fairly recently.

NOAA scientists and their research partners are expanding the atmospheric body of knowledge, shedding new light on the processes that contribute to the world's weather, and developing new tools for predicting it. No one can prevent the weather, but greater understanding of it can help save lives and property throughout the world. NOAA is involved in numerical modeling, assessing information received from satellites and Doppler weather radars (NEXRAD), and sophisticated weather warning and display systems, all leading to improved severe weather forecasts and warnings.

Other research programs focus on the observation and study of the chemical and physical processes of the atmosphere, and detecting the effects of pollution on those processes. They are involved in hurricane research modeling, tornado and thunderstorm modeling, predicting winter and other hazardous weather, aviation weather, weather observing and information systems, understanding air quality, and weather modeling and prediction.

NOAA's hurricane research is aimed at better understanding and predicting tropical cyclones. These investigations involve theoretical studies, computer modeling, and the collection and examination of measurements taken in actual hurricanes. The more progress scientists make toward being able to predict extreme weather events, the more lives can be saved when they occur—such as Hurricane Katrina that struck the southeastern United States in 2006. The ultimate goal is to improve scientific understanding on how and why hurricanes form, strengthen, and dissipate, which will lead to improved forecasting of tropical weather and lessen damage to life and property.

Tornadoes and thunderstorm research is currently being conducted by the National Severe Storms Laboratory (NSSL). NSSL is beginning to test a new type of radar for weather detection called *phased array*, which scans the sky approximately six times faster than the current Doppler radars. They recently made a modification to Doppler radar called *dual polarization*, which will provide meteorologists much more detail about the internal workings of storms than before. NOAA's Environmental Technology Lab studies very low frequency sound waves, or "infrasound," caused by severe storms, earthquakes, and tsunamis. They are exploring if these signals can be used for prediction or detection of tornadoes.

Winter storms can be a tremendous inconvenience or worse, shutting down airports, causing dangerous driving conditions, closing schools, and posing a significant danger to the public. In addition to the hazards of winter weather, many communities must deal with floods, fire weather, lightning and other risky weather conditions. NOAA is conducting research designed to improve the understanding, analysis, and prediction of precipitation and precipitation processes in complex terrain. Scientists are also studying how icing forms within clouds and how the conditions can be detected remotely to assist pilots when flying through these hazardous conditions. Also, in order to assist pilots, research is being conducted in order to be able to generate warnings, forecasts, and weather observations that are more accurate and easier to access. The labs have developed new weather models, radar products, and software.

Better weather observation and information systems are being developed that encompass improved satellite data. Recently, there has been a tremendous expansion in the number of automated weather stations and weather stations overall across the United States. Real-time surface observations will make information available quicker to sectors such as agriculture, energy, transportation, emergency management, fire management, meteorological research, and education.

Research in air quality is also an important field. Air-quality problems are complex, and knowledge of the processes and sources that control pollution formation and distribution is needed to guide the development of policy and management plans. Research areas include laboratory studies, intensive field studies, modeling, and long-term measurement. Data from this research informs policy makers and resource managers about the processes, impacts, and potential solutions.

Weather modeling and prediction models are one of the most important tools for forecasters. These numerical models are comprised of complex mathematical equations that represent the behavior of a physical system, such as the atmosphere. They use millions of numbers that represent weather parameters such as temperature, pressure, and wind. Researchers are involved in refining these models for even faster interpretation and more accurate prediction.

Climate Research

Researchers at NOAA are actively involved in researching the multitude of mechanisms that control climate. These scientists want to improve their ability to predict climate variation in both the short term (cold spells or periods of drought) and over the longer term (centuries and beyond). Research is focusing on carbon levels in the atmosphere and global warming, computer modeling, understanding climate change, climatic prediction, ozone research, Arctic research, and paleoclimatology.

In the geologic history of the Earth, carbon has been cycling among large reservoirs in the land, oceans, and atmosphere. This natural cycling of CO_2 usually takes millions of years to move large amounts from one system to another. According to experts, we are now looking at these changes occurring in the space of centuries or even decades. One of NOAA's major goals is to understand climate variability and change, in order to enhance society's ability to plan and respond. For this reason, NOAA scientists are examining the entire global carbon cycle—including the Earth's atmosphere, fossil fuels, the oceans, and terrestrial ecosystems—to better understand how the carbon cycle works and to help predict how it will act and react in the future.

Climate modeling is another key area of interest for the future. Scientists are interested in the role greenhouse gases play on climate and the impacts of man-made changes to the energy budget. Computer models are essential scientific tools for understanding and predicting natural and human-caused changes in the Earth's climate. Computer modeling attempts to understand the interactions of many components, such as greenhouse warming, atmospheric chemistry, past climates, ocean circulation, and extreme climatic events. Better understanding will come with more research, which in turn will give scientists valuable information about climate change and predictions regarding El Niño, drought cycles, dust bowls, and changing atmospheric circulation patterns. Much of the climate research today has focused on determining whether the human-caused increase in greenhouse gases is the cause of the observed changes in the last century's climate.

NOAA Research has, for many years, played a vital role in studying the ozone layer of the atmosphere, such as in the design of computer models for studying this issue. NOAA researchers build and deploy instruments all over the world to measure ozone, as well as the trace gases and aerosol particles that affect its abundance. A great deal of research is focused on holes in the ozone layer and the resulting depletion. Research in this area is conducted in Antarctica and by using atmospheric models. By successfully monitoring and understanding the characteristics of the ozone layer, better decisions will be made about protecting life on Earth.

Arctic research is also of great interest to scientists. In recent years, decreasing ocean pack ice, increasing air temperatures, thawing permafrost, and redistribution of plants and animals in the delicately balanced Arctic ecosystem indicate that Arctic climate is changing at an unprecedented rate. Scientists today are searching for answers to issues concerning how such changes will impact populations and the quality of life. If scientists can observe and understand Arctic processes, they can provide information to worldwide policy and decision makers. It is important to educate these decision-makers so that dedicated, consistent, and long-term changes occur that lead to the responsible stewardship of these resources. Currently, NOAA's activities in the Arctic are directed toward integration of Arctic observations, advancement of Arctic modeling efforts, improving Arctic satellite observations, providing leadership on Arctic ocean and coastal issues, and providing Arctic air and sea observations that are critical to assessing change in the climate system.

Paleoclimatology is the study of the climate that existed prior to the widespread availability of records of temperature, precipitation, and other instrumental data. NOAA is particularly interested in the climate of the last few thousand years because this is the best-dated, best-sampled part of the past climatic record. This record can help us establish the range of natural climatic variability in a period prior to global-scale human influence. Scientists are interested in understanding about past climates in order to understand the relevant mechanisms. This, in turn, will allow them to further understand what the conditions mean today. They want to know how climate may change in the future and what impacts it will have on life.

Since the paleoclimate record shows that the Earth's climate system is capable of shifting dramatically to a different climate state, changes in the frequency and intensity of extreme events may be a symptom of this process. Understanding these "climate surprises" of the past is critical if we are to avoid the consequences of abrupt climatic change. It is important that scientists study abrupt climate change, as well as changes in the frequency and intensity of the past climate to enable society to prepare for potential future climate change. The study of past climate change also helps us understand how humans influence the Earth's climate system.

The future is open to exploration. The abundance of life on Earth is closely tied to water and atmosphere, which are the lifeblood of Earth's natural systems. Through humans' natural curiosity about the sea and sky, discoveries from the ocean and atmosphere may someday make things possible that were only once dreamed of.

abyssal plain   The vast, flat ocean floor beyond the continental slope and continental rise; it is covered with a thick layer of sediment.

acid rain   Rain with a pH of less than 5.6; results from atmospheric moisture mixing with sulphur and nitrogen oxides emitted from burning fossil fuels or from volcanic activity; may cause damage to buildings, monuments, car finishes, crops, forests, wildlife habitats, and aquatic life.

acidic   Having a pH value of less than 7; acidic liquids are corrosive and sour.

acidity   A characteristic of substances with a pH less than 7; they tend to form acids.

albedo   Solar reflectance; it is a measure of a material's ability to reflect sunlight.

alkaline   Something that has the qualities of a base instead of an acid; its pH is greater than 7.

aquaculture   Farming of plants and animals that live in water, such as fish, shellfish, and algae.

aquifer   A geologic formation that will yield water to a well in sufficient quantities to make the production of water from this formation feasible for beneficial use; permeable layers of underground rock or sand that hold or transmit groundwater below the water table.

archipelago   A group or chain of islands clustered together in a sea or ocean.

artesian water   Groundwater that is under pressure when tapped by a well and is able to rise above the level at which it is first encountered; it may or may not flow out at ground level; the pressure in such an aquifer commonly is called *artesian pressure*, and the formation containing artesian water is an artesian aquifer or confined aquifer.

atolls   These are caused by corals growing on the sides of a volcano that has emerged from the sea; the volcano, worn away by the weather, slowly submerges, and a ring of low-lying coral islands, or atolls, is left.

bay A body of water that is partly enclosed by land (and is usually smaller than a gulf).

black smoker This is a hot, underwater volcanic spring found next to a mid-oceanic ridge; it releases hot water filled with minerals that looks like black smoke pouring from the seafloor.

cape A pointed piece of land that sticks out into a sea, ocean, lake, or river.

carbon monoxide (CO) A colorless, odorless, poisonous gas produced by incomplete burning of carbon-based fuels, including gasoline, oil, and wood; carbon monoxide is also produced from incomplete combustion of many natural and synthetic products; it can cause serious health effects, with death possible from massive exposures.

CFCs (chlorofluorocarbons) These chemicals and some related chemicals have been used in great quantities in industry, for refrigeration and air conditioning, and in consumer products; when released into the air, they rise into the stratosphere where they take part in chemical reactions, which result in reduction of the stratospheric ozone layer that protects the Earth's surface from the harmful effects of radiation from the sun.

Clean Air Act The original Clean Air Act was passed in 1963, but the U.S. national air pollution control program is actually based on the 1970 version of the law; the 1990 Clean Air Act Amendments are the most far-reaching revisions of the 1970 law.

continental shelf The gently sloping shelf along the edges of continents; it ends in a steep slope called the continental slope; sediments dropped at the bottom of the continental slope form the continental rise.

coral reef A structure built in warm waters from the hard remains of small animals called polyps, or corals; there are three kinds of reefs: fringing reefs, barrier reefs, and atolls.

Coriolis effect   The way that the rotation of the Earth makes the winds and ocean currents bend; they bend to the right north of the equator and to the left south of the equator.

cove   A small, horseshoe-shaped body of water along the coast.

deep-sea vent   A crack in the seabed through which hot water and minerals erupt; vents are usually found along mid-ocean ridges; they are sometimes called black or white smokers.

delta   Low, watery land at the mouth of a river formed from the silt, sand, and small rocks that flow downstream and are deposited in the delta; a delta is often shaped like a triangle.

emission   The release of pollutants into the air from a source.

equator   An imaginary circle around the Earth, halfway between the north and south poles.

estuary   Where a river meets the sea or ocean.

evaporation   The process by which water is changed from a liquid into a vapor.

global warming   The gradual rise of the Earth's surface temperature; global warming is believed to be caused by the greenhouse effect and is responsible for changes in global climate patterns and an increase in the near-surface temperature of the Earth. Although global warming has occurred throughout the history of the Earth (the natural greenhouse effect that makes the Earth inhabitable), the term today is most often used in reference to the impacts of human interference and activity.

greenhouse gas   Any gas that absorbs infrared radiation in the atmosphere; greenhouse gases include water vapor, carbon dioxide, methane, nitrous oxide, halogenated fluorocarbons, ozone, perfluorinated carbons, and hydrofluorocarbons.

groundwater   Water that flows or seeps downward and saturates soil or rock, supplying springs and wells; the upper surface of the saturated zone is called the water table.

gulf   A part of the ocean that is partly surrounded by land.

gulf stream   The oceanic current that brings warm Gulf of Mexico water up along the East Coast of the United States and across the Atlantic to the British Isles.

guyot   A seamount whose summit has been worn away by the waves, giving it a flat top.

hazardous air pollutants (HAPs)   Chemicals that cause serious health and environmental effects; health effects include cancer, birth defects, nervous system problems, and death due to massive accidental releases; hazardous air pollutants are released by sources such as chemical plants, dry cleaners, printing plants, and motor vehicles.

hot spring   A spring whose waters are above normal surface temperatures owing to warming by magma beneath the surface.

hurricanes   These are tropical storms that cause devastation as they move away from the equator; hurricanes are also known as cyclones and typhoons.

hydrologic cycle   The cyclic transfer of water vapor from the Earth's surface via evapotranspiration into the atmosphere; from the atmosphere via precipitation back to Earth; and through runoff into streams, rivers, and lakes, and ultimately into the oceans.

hydrology   The science encompassing the behavior of water as it occurs in the atmosphere, on the surface of the ground, and underground.

hydrothermal vent   A vent ejecting a stream of hot, or hydrothermal, solutions.

hypoxic   Containing very little or decreased oxygen.

intertidal   Of, or pertaining to, a shore zone bounded by the levels of low and high tide.

lagoon   A shallow stretch of seawater partly or completely separated from the open ocean by a narrow strip of land, such as a reef or a spit.

latitude   The angular distance north or south from the equator to a particular location; the equator has a latitude of 0°; the North Pole has a latitude of 90°N; the South Pole has a latitude of 90°S.

longitude   The angular distance east or west from the north-south line that passes through Greenwich, England, to a particular location. Greenwich, England, has a longitude of 0°; the farther east or west of Greenwich, the greater the longitude is; the Midway Islands, in the Pacific Ocean, have a longitude of 180° (they are on the opposite side of the globe from Greenwich).

marsh   A type of freshwater, brackish water, or saltwater wetland that is found along rivers, ponds, lakes, and coasts; marsh plants grow up out of the water.

mid-ocean ridge   A long, narrow chain of underwater mountains that has formed where two of the Earth's plates moved apart and magma spilled out onto the ocean floor.

nitrogen oxides (NO$_x$)   A common air pollutant; nitrogen oxides are produced from burning fuels, including gasoline and coal; nitrogen oxides are smog formers, which react with volatile organic compounds to form smog; they are also major components of acid rain.

ocean   A large body of salt water that surrounds a continent; oceans cover more than two-thirds of the Earth's surface.

ocean basin   A great depression in the Earth's crust that is filled with ocean or sea; an ocean basin does not include the continental shelf.

ocean current   A "river" of water flowing in the oceans; there are two main types of currents: surface currents, which carry warm water from the equator to the poles, and deep-water currents, which carry cold water from the poles to the equator.

ocean trench   A long, narrow valley under the sea, usually near a continental shelf, where old ocean floor is being pushed down inside the Earth.

oceanographer   A person who studies the science of the oceans.

ozone   A colorless gas with a pungent odor that has the molecular form O$_3$; it is found in two layers of the atmosphere, the stratosphere and the troposphere; in the stratosphere, ozone provides a protective layer shielding the Earth from the potentially harmful health effects of the sun's ultraviolet radiation; at ground level (the troposphere), ozone is a pollutant that affects human health and the environment and contributes to the formation of smog.

particulate matter (PM)   A common air pollutant; particulate matter includes dust, soot, and other tiny bits of solid materials that are released into and move around in the atmosphere; they are produced by the burning of diesel fuels, incineration of garbage, mixing and application of fertilizers and pesticides, road construction, industrial processes (such as steelmaking, mining operations, and agricultural burning), and operation of fireplaces and woodstoves; they cause eye, nose, and throat irritation and other health problems.

peninsula   A body of land that is surrounded by water on three sides.

plankton   Tiny creatures that live in the sea; they can be phytoplankton (plants) or zooplankton (animals).

pollutants (pollution)   Unwanted chemicals or other materials found in the air; pollutants can harm health, the environment, and property; many air pollutants occur as gases or vapors, but some are very tiny solid particles such as dust, smoke, or soot.

pond   A small body of water surrounded by land; a pond is smaller than a lake.

recycled water   Water that is used more than one time before it passes back into the natural hydrologic system, generally by the same user, or for similar purposes.

ridges   Mid-oceanic ridges occur where two plates move apart and ridges form from the cooling of the molten rock, which is forced up from the center of the Earth.

river   A large, flowing body of water that usually empties into a sea or ocean.

runoff   Water (originating as precipitation) that flows across surfaces rather than soaking in; it eventually enters a water body and may pick up and carry a variety of pollutants.

scuba   Jacques Cousteau invented scuba, the self-contained underwater breathing apparatus, in the 1940s; it allows people to breathe underwater for a long time but limits the scuba diver to 165 feet (50 meters) of depth.

sea   A large body of salty water that is often connected to an ocean; a sea may be partly or completely surrounded by land.

sea farming   This is the intensive growing of seafood such as salmon, seaweed, and oysters; this is a very productive process and much better than wasteful fishing techniques.

sea level   The average level of the sea around the world.

seamount   This is a mountain under the sea.

sound   A wide inlet of the sea or ocean that is parallel to the coastline; it often separates a coastline from a nearby island.

strait   A narrow body of water that connects two larger bodies of water.

swamp   A type of freshwater wetland that has spongy, muddy land and a lot of water; many trees and shrubs grow in swamps.

tide   The alternate rise and fall of the surface of oceans, seas, and the bays, rivers, and so forth, that are connected with them; caused by the attraction of the moon and sun; the tide occurs once or twice in each period of 24 hours and 50 minutes.

trenches   Deep areas of the ocean seabed that are caused by one crustal plate slipping beneath another.

tributary   A stream or river that flows into a larger river.

tsunami   Very powerful waves that wreak havoc and leave devastation in their wake; caused by underwater earthquakes or landslides.

upwelling   The rise of cold nutrient-rich water to the ocean's surface that replaces warmer water that has been blown from the coast by the wind; this usually creates good fisheries.

urban heat island effect   A measurable increase in ambient urban air temperatures resulting primarily from the replacement of vegetation with buildings, roads, and other heat-absorbing infrastructure; the heat island effect can result in significant temperature differences between rural and urban areas.

waterfall   A river that falls steeply off a landform or dam.

watershed   An area drained by a river.

wetland   An area of land that is often covered or saturated with water; the soil in wetlands is often low in oxygen; wetland plants are adapted to life in wet soil; there are many types of wetlands, including swamp, slough, fen, bog, marsh, moor, muskeg, peatland, bottomland, mire, wet meadow, and riparian area.

FURTHER READING

Arms, Karen. *Environmental Science*. Austin, Tex.: Holt, Rinehart, and Winston, Inc.,1996.

Bouwer, Herman. *Groundwater Hydrology*. New York: McGraw Hill Book Company, 1978.

Chiras, Daniel D. *Environmental Science, High School Edition*. Menlo Park, Calif.: Addison-Wesley, 1989.

Cunningham, William P., and Barbara Woodworth Saigo. *Environmental Science: A Global Concern*. Dubuque, Iowa: Wm. C. Brown Publishers, 1997.

Knopman, Debra S., and Richard A. Smith. "Twenty Years of the Clean Water Act." *Environment*, January/February 1993.

Nebel, Bernard J., and Richard T. Wright. *Environmental Science: The Way the World Works,* 4th ed. Upper Saddle River, N.J.: Prentice-Hall, 1993.

WEB SITES

American Geological Institute
http://www.agiweb.org

American Shore & Beach Preservation Association
http://www.asbpa.org

Coasts, Oceans, Ports & Rivers Institute of the American Society of Civil Engineers
http://www.coprinstitute.org

Coastal Services Center
http://www.csc.noaa.gov

Environmental System Research Institute (GIS)
http://www.esri.com

The Geological Society of America
http://www.geology.com

National Oceanic and Atmospheric Administration
http://www.noaa.gov

The U.S. Department of the Interior Minerals Management Service
http://www.mms.gov

The U.S. Geological Survey
http://www.usgs.gov

A

Abyssal plain, 37
Acid rain
  control, 152
  effects, 95, 137, 151–152
Aesthetic values, 128
  of water, 44, 70, 119
  of wetlands, 120–121
Air quality
  effects on, 26, 93, 128, 151–152
  indoor, 152–153
  issues, 73, 93–98, 144–147
  management, 72, 137
  measurement, 21
  models, 98
  research, 177, 182–185
Air Quality Index (AQI), 21
Air Resources Laboratory (ARL), 93
AIS. *See* Aquatic invasive species
Alginate, 59–60
Amazon River, 13, 61
  drainage basin, 17
Antarctica
  ice caps, 7, 17, 51, 164–165
  ozone, 167–168
  preservation, 154, 164–165, 167
  research, 165, 186
AQI. *See* Air Quality Index
Aquatic invasive species (AIS)
  threats of, 178–180
Aquatic systems
  resources, 61–64, 66
Aquifers, 2
  bedrock, 10
  recreational, 65
  water yield from, 9–11, 49, 52–54,
    61, 101
ARL. *See* Air Resources Laboratory
Arctic Ocean, 40, 61
Asthma, 21, 144
Atlantic Ocean, 40–41, 172
Atmospheric resources
  concepts of, 1–27
  conditions today, 35, 37–40
  conservation, 154–168

critical cycles, 47–49, 51–58
development of, 73–98
future, 169–187
importance of, 1, 119–136, 170
influence of, 28–45
interaction with water, 23, 25,
  134
land use effects on, 2
management of, 72, 137–153
and the ocean, 18, 23, 25, 40, 57, 69,
  76–77
prehistoric condition of, 28–29,
  31–33
quality, 26–27
use and impact of, 99–128
water storage, 5, 14–16, 47–49
Aurora, 135

B

Baikal Lake, 12
Beaufort Sea, 75
Bioacoustics, 131–132
Biospheres, 47
  and carbon cycle, 55–57
  effects on climate, 26, 101
  extinction, 31
  and the nitrogen cycle, 57–59
  pollution effects on, 93,
    105–107
  in the sea, 37–39, 58–61, 65, 68,
    103
  today, 35, 37–40
  waste and remains, 55, 57, 74, 76
  and wetlands, 120, 122
Black smokers, 173

C

Capillary action, 4
Carbon
  cycle, 46–47, 54–57, 181
  emissions, 56, 94–95, 144–148
  forms of, 56, 76
  management options, 57
  poisoning, 112
  sequestration, 56–57

Carbon dioxide, 29
  absorption, 55
  atmospheric levels of, 56–57,
    117–118, 185
  exchange, 55
  release of, 35, 38, 56, 134
Carlsbad Caverns, 35
Carrageenan, 59–60
Caspian Sea, 13
Cave development, 35
Cellular respiration, 55
Center for Coastal Environmental Health
    and Biomolecular Research, 101
CFCs. See Chlorofluorocarbons
Chlorofluorocarbons (CFCs), 167–68
Civilization
  development, 44–45, 58
Clean Air Act (1970)
  amendments, 146, 151, 167
  regulations, 93–94, 97, 144
Climate
  around the world, 26, 164–165, 167
  buffering, 69
  defined, 26
  effects on, 3, 25, 101, 117–118, 134, 161
  research, 26, 31–34, 130,
    134–135, 177, 181, 185–187
  tropical, 84
Coastal
  communities, 103, 108, 124, 126,
    164, 170
  dynamic equilibrium, 103
  erosion, 101, 103, 120, 134, 172, 175
  impacts of, 58, 65–66, 99,
    101–104
  management, 101, 137, 142, 178
  nourishment, 104
  research, 177–182, 186
  wetlands, 119–122, 142
  winds, 68–70, 73
Community
  coastal, 103, 142, 179
  fishing, 104
  water supplies, 53–54, 62

Concentrating solar power (CSP)
    technology, 77–78
Condensation, 47, 49
Conduction, 23, 25
Congo River, 13
Continental shelf, 37
Convention, 23, 25
Coral reefs
  bleaching, 124
  creation, 122
  deposits, 34–35, 37
  future of, 160
  medicinal resources, 129–130, 162,
    164, 179
  polyps, 38, 122
  predators and diseases, 124, 161
  preservation and restoration, 38,
    125–126, 135, 154, 160–164
  research, 124–125, 134, 162, 164
  species, 122, 124–125, 162, 164
  vitality of, 119
  vulnerability, 124–125, 170
Coral Reef Conservation Act, 160
Coriolis effect, 25
CSP. See Concentrating solar power
    technology

D
Death Valley, 5
Density
  of water, 4–6
Drinking water
  and government regulations, 5, 63,
    138–141
  security and counter-terrorism,
    141
  supply of, 2, 9, 61–62, 113, 119,
    137–138, 154
  treatment plants, 54, 63, 100,
    139–141
Droughts
  cycles, 185–186
  effects of, 6, 51, 62, 101, 114–115,
    155

E

Earthquakes
  effects of, 113, 115
  research, 184
Ecology
  cycles, 46
  forecasting, 178
  study of, 131, 134
Ecosystems
  biodiversity, 31, 41, 64–67, 88,
    121–122, 124–125, 131–132, 135,
    160, 164, 167, 179–181
  effects on, 1, 68, 78, 101, 118, 126,
    128, 154, 167, 173, 175, 186
  fragile, 38, 106
  research, 130–131
Education, 130–136
EEZ. *See* Exclusive economic zone
Electromagnetic radiation, 136
El Niño, 134, 186
Employment, 130–136
Energy Department
  research, 56–57, 74, 76, 91–92
Energy heat transfer, 69
  conduction, 23, 25
  convention, 23, 25
  radiation, 23, 25, 134
Energy Policy Act (2005), 75
Environmental Protection Agency (EPA)
  and fishing, 58, 103
  and the greenhouse effects, 118
  and ground water resources, 11–12, 100
  and the ozone, 21, 168
  and pollution, 93–98, 102, 105, 107,
    144, 146–150, 152
  and water conservation, 155
  and water resources, 6–7, 13, 16, 54,
    62, 138, 140–142
Environmental Technology Lab,
    183–184
EPA. *See* Environmental Protection
    Agency
Equator, 25
  currents, 40–42, 44

  doldrums, 42
  widest point, 39
Estuaries, 13
  coastal, 66, 103
  functions of, 14–15, 65
  resources, 61, 64
Evaporation, 3
  process of, 47–49, 52, 67, 69, 77, 151, 157
  research, 48
Evapotranspiration, 47, 49
Exclusive economic zone (EEZ), 74
Extreme heat
  related illnesses, 114–115
Exxon Valdez oil spills, 106

F

Farmlands, 122
  effects of, 26–27, 102, 124, 168
  irrigations, 27, 52, 100, 138, 151,
    157, 160
  research, 182
  runoff, 139
  sources, 61
FDA. *See* Food and Drug
    Administration
Fishing, 2
  commercial, 65, 78, 100, 120
  communities, 104
  effects of, 124–125, 142, 178
  farms, 60–61, 137
  overfishing, 101, 103–105, 132,
    134–135, 161
  sources, 58–61, 65–68, 182
Fish and Wildlife Service, 67
Floods
  causes, 112
  control, 64, 66, 122
  effects of, 101, 112–113, 115
  flash, 178
  generating systems, 85
  mosquitoes, 112
  storage, 120–121
Food and Drug Administration (FDA)
  standards, 140

Food resources
  impacts on, 58–61, 66, 103–104, 119
  research, 100
  and wetlands, 120–121
Fossil fuel
  combustion, 56–57, 117–118
  research, 76–77, 186
Freshwater
  composition, 5
  distribution, 6
  extraction, 175, 177
  lakes, 12
  resources, 9, 14–15, 47, 51–52, 62,
    64, 84, 119, 165
  uses, 99–101, 156
  wetlands, 119–122

G

Geologists, 31
Geothermal resources, 73, 89–90
Giardia, 140
Global challenges, 169–170
  average temperatures, 117
  working together, 17
Global Coral Reef Monitoring
    Network, 124
Global warming, 69
  contributions to, 95, 99, 117–118,
    149
  effects of, 135, 185
Gondwanaland, 165
Great Plains, 108
Great Salt Lake, 13
Greenhouse effect
  gases, 20, 99, 117–118, 135,
    149–150, 185–186
  and global climate change,
    117–118
  research, 20–21, 26, 117–118, 148
Greenland
  ice caps, 7, 17
Groundwater
  discharge, 11, 47, 49, 52, 63
  recharge, 9, 11, 63–64

  reservoirs, 5–7, 9–12, 14–15, 47, 49,
    52–54, 61–62
  roles of, 9, 31
  runoff, 9, 49
  table, 49
  vadose, 9, 15
Gulf of Mexico, 68, 75, 103
Gulf Stream, 23, 85
Guyots, 37

H

Health effects
  and air quality, 93–96, 144,
    146–147, 152–153
  and extreme heat, 114–115
  and the ozone, 21–22
  and tsunamis, 113
  and water quality, 138
Health and Human Services
    Department (DHS)
  recommendations, 116
  reports on severe weather, 108–109,
    113, 115–116
Heat island effect, 137, 148
  maximums, 149
  reduction strategies, 150–151
Hot spring, 89
Humidity
  effects on climate, 26, 49
Hurricanes, 15
  effects of, 101, 103, 105, 109,
    111–113, 115, 134, 178
  forecasts, 181, 183
  safety measures, 75
Hydrocarbons, 74
Hydroelectric power, 73
  generation, 84, 86–88, 139
Hydrogen
  and water, 4
Hydrology
  and water resources, 5–6, 178
Hydrothermal vents
  exploration of, 170–171, 173,
    178–179

I

Ice caps and glaciers
  formation, 31, 33–34
  and methane, 76
  runoff, 52, 63, 112, 152
  transportation, 61
  and volcanic eruptions, 112–113
  water storage in, 5–7, 14–15, 47, 49,
    51, 64, 164–165
Indian Ocean, 40–41
Industry
  effects on ecosystem, 78
  pollutants, 26, 54, 94, 96, 102,
    144–145, 147–148, 151, 170
  and sand and gravel, 70
  and water use, 2, 61, 100, 139
Infiltration
  and the water cycle, 47, 52–53
International Coral Reef Initiative, 125

L

Lakes
  acidic, 152
  ancient, 34
  edges of, 119
  freezing, 2–3
  fresh, 12–15
  and groundwater, 11
  research, 177–182
  salt, 12–15
  uses, 2, 55, 67, 139, 177
  water storage, 5–6, 17, 48, 52, 54, 64,
    101
Land, 13, 47
  coastal impacts of, 101–104
  development, 29, 31, 34
  drainage, 14, 52
  erosion, 54, 125, 140–141, 160,
    171–172
  interaction with oceans, 25
  managers, 2, 17, 58, 102, 128, 160
  permeable, 9–10
  runoff, 47, 49, 51–52
  use, 2, 26–27, 99, 101–104, 141

Lead
  emissions, 96
Legionnaires' disease, 153

M

Marine biodiversity
  animals, 14, 68, 128–129, 131, 133,
    135, 170
  aquaculture, 60–61, 75, 100–101,
    121–122, 128–129, 131–132, 142,
    175, 178–180, 182
  conservation, 131
  effects on, 68, 86, 133
  medicinal resources, 129–130
  and overfishing, 101, 103–105, 132,
    134–135
  pollution, 134
Marsh grasses, 15, 103
Methane hydrates, 74
  atmospheric levels, 117
  recovery, 76–77
Mineral Management Service
  research, 70, 74–77
Mineral resources, 67–68, 119
Mississippi River, 7, 13

N

NAAQS. *See* National Ambient Air
  Quality Standards
Nantucket Sound, 81
National Ambient Air Quality
  Standards (NAAQS), 98
National Environmental Policy Act
  (1969), 138
National Oceanic and Atmospheric
  Administration (NOAA), 58, 93,
  101
  goals of, 185
  research, 177–183, 185–186
National Pollutant Discharge
  Elimination System (NPDES),
  138
National Primary Drinking Water
  Regulations (NPDWRs), 6, 138

National Renewable Energy
    Laboratory, 84
National Severe Storms Laboratory
    (NSSL), 178, 183–184
National Weather Service, 112
Navigation, 44–45
Nile River, 44
Nitrogen
    cycle, 46–47, 57–58
    denitrification, 58
    nitrification, 58
    oxide, 95, 117, 148, 151–152
    properties of, 17
NOAA. *See* National Oceanic and
    Atmospheric Administration
Nonrenewable resources,
        46–72
    energy, 74
North American Great Lakes, 12
North Sea, 68
NPDWRs. *See* National Primary
    Drinking Water Regulations
NSSL. *See* National Severe Storms
    Laboratory

O

Oceans
    basins, 172
    circulation, 134
    and the climate, 3, 69, 134
    currents, 23, 40–42, 44, 69, 77,
        85–86, 101
    desalination, 63
    development of, 34, 73–98
    distribution, 1, 7, 14–15, 17, 31
    effects on the atmosphere, 18, 23, 25,
        40, 57, 69, 134
    energy, 73–77, 85–86
    evaporation, 48–49, 55, 67, 69, 77
    formation, 28–29, 171
    and groundwater, 11
    health, 72
    interaction with land, 25, 101
    medicinal resources, 129–130
    mining, 172–173, 175, 177

noise, 134
    research, 74, 77, 85–86, 134, 167,
        169–171, 173, 175, 177–182
    resources, 58–61, 63–64, 67–68, 70–
        71, 73–75, 90, 119, 169–173, 175,
        177–179, 187
    seabed, 37–39, 67–68, 74–77,
        103–104, 172
    tides, 68, 73–74, 77, 84–85, 103
    water storage, 5–6, 47–48, 52
    waves, 73–74, 77, 81, 83–84, 101,
        103, 108, 113, 120
Oceanographers, 165
Ocean Thermal Energy Conversion
    (OTEC), 83–84
OCS. *See* Outer Continental Shelf
Oil spills
    effects of, 68, 75, 99, 105–108, 169
    recovery, 106–108, 142
OTEC. *See* Ocean Thermal Energy
    Conversion
Outer Continental Shelf (OCS), 171
Oxygen
    in the atmosphere, 18–20, 29
    dependent life-form, 69
    dissolved, 148
    production, 69
    properties of, 17
    and water, 4, 66, 138
Ozone, 17
    chemical structure of, 19
    concentrations, 21–22, 186
    depletion, 124, 165, 167–168
    distribution, 18
    formation, 20, 22–23
    ground-level, 22, 98, 146
    precursors, 22
    repair, 71–72, 154, 167–168
    and smog, 21

P

Pacific Ocean, 39, 41, 172
Paleoclimatology
    research, 185–187
Pangaea, 29

Persian Gulf, 68
Petroleum and natural gas
  refineries, 96, 100
  sources, 58, 68, 71, 74–76, 119, 171
Photonic technology, 77–78
Physiology, 131–132, 165
Plankton
  fertilization, 57
  photosynthetic, 15, 38, 57, 68–69
  thriving, 37
Plants
  and carbon cycle, 55
  deaths, 57–58, 74, 76
  development, 29
  and energy, 29
  growth, 35, 165
  mineralization, 56
  and nitrogen cycle, 57–58
  and photosynthesis, 55, 68
  pollution effects on, 93, 101
  sea, 37–38, 58–59, 67–68, 129
  transpiration, 48–49, 52
  water supply, 9, 49, 52, 54
Plate tectonics theory
  evidence of, 29, 31, 34–35
Polarity, 4
Pollution
  air, 21–22, 27, 54, 71, 93–95, 97–98, 137, 144–53
  animal waste, 26–27
  control, 137, 144–46
  indoor, 137, 152–53
  industrial and commercial, 26, 54, 102, 137, 144–145, 147–148, 170
  lead, 96
  mobile sources of, 146–48
  prevention, 75, 97–98, 147–148, 160
  research, 26
  sediment, 26, 54, 65
  thermal, 137, 148–151
  water, 26–27, 38, 54, 63, 67, 71, 87, 93, 124, 128, 134, 139–42, 154, 157, 161, 164, 169–170, 181

Ponds
  uses, 2
Power generation, 68–69
Precipitation
  critical role of, 1–2, 23, 29, 32–33, 63
  effects on, 42, 77, 115
  and groundwater, 9, 16
  heavy, 112, 152
  and water cycle, 47, 49, 52–54
Prehistoric conditions
  atmospheric, 28–29, 31
  evidence of, 31–35
  water, 28–29, 31
Properties, of atmosphere
  gases, 17–23, 25, 29, 55–57, 108, 117–118, 146, 185
  layers, 17–20, 25, 146, 165, 167–168
  water vapor, 17–18, 23, 47–49, 54, 95, 117
Properties, of water
  capillary action, 4
  density, 4–6
  heat capacity, 3
  natural states of, 1–5, 47–48, 55
  polarity, 4
  surface tension, 4
Public Health Security and
  Bioterrorism Preparedness and
  Response Act (2002), 141

R

Radiation, 23, 25
  unhealthy levels, 71
Recreation, 128, 146
  fishing, 78
  rivers, 143–144
  scuba diving, 45, 70, 126, 128, 161
  and water use, 2, 45, 64–65, 70, 76, 100, 119, 126, 128, 131, 142, 172
  and wetlands, 120–121
Renewable resources, 47–72
  forms of energy, 27, 74, 89–90, 118
  impacts on, 54, 68
  research on, 46

Research, 130–136
  on climate changes, 26, 31–34, 130,
    134–135, 165, 177, 181, 185–187
  on coral reefs, 124–125, 135, 162,
    164
  and education, 75, 119–121,
    130–136, 178, 182
  on energy, 77–78, 81, 83, 91–92,
    135–136
  on food sources, 100
  future, 169, 177–187
  on greenhouse effects, 20–21, 26,
    117–118, 135, 149, 185–186
  on medicinal resources, 129–130
  on methane hydrates, 76–77
  on neuroscience, 130
  ocean, lake and coastal, 74, 85–86,
    131–135, 167, 169–171, 173, 175,
    177–182, 187
  and the ozone layer, 18, 167–168,
    185–186
  on paleoclimatology, 185–187
  on pollution, 26, 54, 134, 144, 152,
    177, 181, 184
  on prehistoric conditions, 28–29,
    31–33
  on renewable resources, 46, 48
  on water resources, 6, 13, 17, 76, 138
  on weather, 87, 134, 177, 181–185
Rivers and streams, 13
  acidic, 152
  civilizations around, 44
  edges of, 119
  and electricity, 86–87
  flooding, 178
  freezing, 2–3
  and groundwater, 11
  runoff, 63
  uses, 2, 99, 137, 139
  water storage, 5–6, 13, 15, 17, 52,
    64–65, 67, 101
  and wetlands, 122
  wild and scenic, 142–144
Rocky Mountains, 108

S

Safe Drinking Water Act (1974)
  passing of, 6, 63, 138, 140
Saltwater lakes
  resources, 12–15
Sand and gravel, 70
  aquifers, 9–11
  resources, 134
  from seabed, 103–104, 172
Scott, Steven, 177
Seabed
  continental shelf, 37–38, 77, 171
  resources, 67–68, 74, 76, 103–104,
    172–173
  ridges, 37
  species, 37, 39
  trenches, 37
Seamounts, 37
Seawater
  components, 5, 13–15
Seaweed
  agarose, 129
  calcium alginate, 129–130
  irish moss, 129
  phycobiliproteins, 129
Sea World Parks
  research institute, 131–134
Settlement
  historical, 121
  permanent, 44–45
  population density, 53, 101
  ports and harbors, 44–45
SIPs. *See* State implementation plans
Solar energy
  and greenhouse effect, 117–118
  and the ozone, 22–23
  research, 77–78
  and ultraviolet radiation, 18–20, 25,
    70, 73, 77–78, 83, 124, 136, 167
  ultraviolet wavelengths, 25
Springs, 47
  and groundwater, 11, 63
  thermal, 53, 90
State implementation plans (SIPs), 97

Sulfur dioxide
  pollutants, 95–96, 151–152
Surface tension, 4

T
Thermal energy, 74, 83–84
Tidal energy, 77
  ebb, 85
  turbines, 84–85
Tornadoes
  effects of, 108–111
  research, 183–184
Tourism, 70, 128
  around water, 44, 70, 119, 126, 142
  effects of, 124, 126–127, 131,
    161–162, 170
Transportation
  and fossil fuels, 27, 146–148
  routes, 44
  and water use, 2, 61, 119, 142
Tsunami
  effects of, 108, 112–114, 181
  research program, 181, 184

U
United Nations
  agencies, 104
  environment programs, 104
United States Geological Survey
    (USGS), 6
  research, 29

V
VOCs. *See* Volatile organic compounds
Volatile organic compounds (VOCs),
  98

W
Wastewater
  management, 137, 141–142,
    154–156, 169
Water resources
  acidity, 35
  concepts of, 1–27

conditions today, 35, 37–40
conservation, 101, 154–168
critical cycles, 47–49, 51–58
distribution, 1, 6–17, 28–29, 31
future research, 9, 169–187
importance of, 1–2, 119–136
influence of, 28–45
interaction with atmosphere, 23, 25
land use effects on, 2
management of, 2, 72, 100, 137–153,
    160, 178
prehistoric conditions, 28–29, 31–35
temperatures, 42, 44
use and impact of, 99–128
Water budget
  components, 16–17, 64
Water conservation, 154–160
  recycle, 60
Water cycle, 46
  and atmosphere, 16–17
  components of, 47–49, 51–54, 67,
    181
Water Pollution Control Act (1972),
    138
Water quality, 27
  effects on, 26, 53–54, 95, 101, 128
  improvement, 120–121
  management, 137–142
  standards, 5, 137
  testing, 67, 138
Watersheds, 17
  management practices, 125, 137, 139
Wave energy
  commercial, 81, 83
  research, 81, 83
Weather and emergency preparedness
  atmosphere levels, 18
  averages, 26
  effects on, 3, 42, 99, 145
  extreme heat, 3, 108, 114–115
  floods, 112–113, 115
  hurricanes15, 75, 101, 103, 105,
    111–113, 115, 134, 178, 181, 183
  modeling, 183–184

Weather and emergency preparedness
    (*Continued*)
  research, 87, 177, 181–185
  tornadoes, 108–111, 115, 183–184
  tsunami, 108, 112–114, 181, 184
  winter storms, 3, 112, 115–116, 184
Wetlands, 11
  artificial, 100
  coastal, 65–66, 103, 119–122, 142
  conservation and preservation,
    125
  freshwater, 52, 119, 119–122
  habitats, 67
  importance of, 65, 67, 119–122
  resources, 61
  riparian areas, 67
Wild and Scenic River Act (1968)
  river classes, 142–144

Wind energy, 73, 95
  currents, 42, 68, 77
  and electricity, 78, 81
  patterns, 42, 101
  and pollution, 145
  powered generators, 69, 91–92
  research, 78, 81, 84
  speed, 103, 105, 115–116, 118
  trade, 42
  turbines, 78, 81, 84, 86, 90–92
Winter storms, 115–116
  research, 184
World Energy Council, 83
World Health Organization
    Committee, 153

Y
Yellowstone National Park, 89

JULIE KERR CASPER holds B.S., M.S., and Ph.D. degrees in earth science with an emphasis on natural resource conservation. She has worked for the United States Bureau of Land Management (BLM) for nearly 30 years and is primarily focused on practical issues concerning the promotion of a healthier, better-managed environment for both the short- and long-term. She has also had extensive experience teaching middle school and high school students over the past 20 years. She has taught classes, instructed workshops, given presentations, and led field trips and science application exercises. She is the author of several award-winning novels, articles, and stories.